DRIED FLOWERS

FOR ALL SEASONS

Creating the Fresh-Flower Look Year-Round

DRIED FLOWERS

FOR ALL SEASONS

JAN AND MICHAEL GERTLEY

The Taunton Press

Publisher: Jim Childs

Associate Publisher: Helen Albert

Assistant Editor: Jennifer Renjilian

Copy Editor: Diane Sinitsky

Designer/Layout Artist: Amy Bernard Russo

Photographer: Michael Gertley

Illustrator: Jan Gertley

Indexer: Harriet Hodges

Taunton
BOOKS & VIDEOS

for fellow enthusiasts

Printed in the United States of America
10 9 8 7 6 5 4 3 2 I

The Taunton Press, Inc., 63 South Main Street, PO Box 5506
Newtown, CT 06470-5506
e-mail: tp@taunton.com

Distributed by Publishers Group West

Library of Congress Cataloging-in-Publication Data
Gertley, Jan.
      Dried flowers for all seasons : creating the fresh-flower look year-round /
Jan and Michael Gertley.
             p.   cm.
     Includes index.
     ISBN I-56I58-285-9
      I. Dried flower arrangement. 2. Flower gardening. 3. Flowers—Drying. 4. Seasons.
I. Gertley, Michael. II. Title
SB449.3.D7G46   1999
745.92—dc2I   99-32130
                                              CIP

*"Flowers have spoken to me more
than I can tell in written words."*
—*Lydia M. Child (1842)*

CONTENTS

ACKNOWLEDGMENTS

We would like to thank our family and friends for their unwavering support and understanding. To BJ—thanks for lending us a helping hand. We love you all!

Our thanks and appreciation also extend to the wonderful staff at The Taunton Press, including Helen Albert, Jennifer Renjilian, Amy Bernard Russo, Carolyn Mandarano, Rosalie Vaccaro, and Diane Sinitsky. Their combined talents and hours of work helped make this book a reality.

INTRODUCTION

The words "dried flowers" and "everlastings" often bring to mind the small, papery petals of straw-flowers and statice. These plants are colorful and dry easily, but they lack the irresistible appeal of large, freshly cut peonies, lilies, lilacs, and hyacinths. We wanted the best of both worlds—a wide assortment of dried flowers that maintained their fresh appearance.

Years ago, we became interested in growing flowers for drying when our search for quality dried materials left us empty-handed. We decided to grow a small dried-flower garden in our backyard and experiment with various drying techniques. Our small plot of land produced an abundant harvest that we hung from rafters, dried in silica gel, and preserved with glycerin.

Feeling sure that other people were having the same trouble finding vibrant dried flowers, we embarked on a plan to grow flowers commercially. The following spring we rented a half-acre of land from a local farmer, including the loft of his barn. By summer's end, the loft was overflowing with flowers—by fall our inventory was sold out.

That first successful season marked the beginning of a career in dried flowers that lasted many years. After four seasons of growing flowers on rented land, we moved to a rural farm where we expanded the business. Our constant goal was to produce vibrant, fresh-looking dried flowers. Our years of growing, harvesting, drying, and arranging dried flowers culminated in this book: *Dried Flowers for All Seasons.*

Most flowers suitable for drying are easy to grow. A small garden space will produce all the flowers and foliage you need to make beautiful, long-lasting arrangements. This book will take you step-by-step through the entire process—from creating a garden plan and starting your own seedlings to harvesting and drying a wide variety of plant materials. Make any of the 24 seasonal arrangements presented in this book, or use them as inspiration to create your own original designs.

Whether you are a flower gardener wanting to preserve the beauty of your garden or a dried-flower arranger wanting to grow your own materials, *Dried Flowers for All Seasons* will help you capture and preserve the fleeting beauty of flowers.

PART ONE

CREATING THE
FRESH LOOK

Chapter 1

Growing

It's easy to create a beautiful flower garden filled with plants that are suitable for drying. Grow a colorful garden this summer and dry the blooms for continued enjoyment all winter long.

D ried flowers are available in most craft stores, floral shops, and through mail-order catalogs. However, it is sometimes difficult to find a good selection of high-quality materials at reasonable prices. Without a doubt, the best way to obtain colorful, fresh-looking dried materials is to grow them yourself—and that's half the fun! Although growing your own plants from seed requires an investment of time, it's far less expensive than purchasing dried flowers from a store.

This chapter will guide you step-by-step from plant selection and garden design through planting and seedling care, garden maintenance, and finally harvesting. A small plot of land and a desire to get your hands dirty is the first step to filling your home with beautiful dried arrangements year-round.

PLANT SELECTION

Growing flowers that are suitable for drying is easy, but selecting the right plants to grow requires some careful consideration. You must decide whether you will grow only annuals or a combination of annuals, perennials, and bulbs. You also need to make sure your garden can supply the variety of plant materials necessary for arranging, such as focal point flowers, filler materials, and foliage.

Comprised mainly of annuals, this garden bed includes amaranth, ornamental grasses, zinnias, love-in-a-mist, starflower, and sunflowers.

Annuals

Annuals are the mainstays of a dried-flower garden. Most are easy to grow, bloom profusely, and are ready to harvest by summer's end. It's possible to grow a garden comprised solely of annuals and have enough variety in the plant materials to create spectacular dried arrangements (all within a matter of months).

We're all familiar with the common everlastings such as strawflowers and statice, but there's a host of annuals that dry just as well, including asters, marigolds, and zinnias. Because annuals complete their life cycle in one season, they offer uncommon freedom in garden design. Their lack of permanence means you can redesign your garden every year. To improve your planting schemes, keep notes on which plant combinations worked well and which did not.

Perennials and biennials

Although it's possible to create an entire dried-flower garden with annuals, you would miss out on all the wonderful colors, shapes, and textures that perennials

Delphinium, liatris, and purple coneflower are among the many perennials suitable for drying.

Flowering bulbs like tulips and hyacinths are a delightful surprise in dried-flower arrangements.

and biennials provide. For example, your garden would be void of bright orange Chinese lanterns, the tall spires of delphinium, and the spiny, thistlelike blooms of sea holly.

Perennials and biennials produce foliage their first year from seed and bloom in their second. At the end of the second season, biennials die, but perennials live on. Perennials may live for many years, so you should anticipate their spreading growth and space them accordingly. Like furniture, they can be moved and rearranged; however it's a large, time-consuming job.

Bulbs

Seeing perfectly preserved hyacinths, daffodils, or tulips in a dried arrangement is an unexpected delight. Bulbs are not often thought of as dried flowers because it takes time and patience to preserve their delicate blooms.

In the garden, spring-flowering bulbs are perfect for tucking into spots where summer-flowering

plants will hide their dying foliage. Also, they are ideal for deck or patio containers—saving precious growing space in your garden.

Types of plant materials

Make a shopping list before you purchase the seeds and bulbs for your dried-flower garden. You'll need a variety of plant colors, textures, shapes, and forms to ultimately create unique and interesting arrangements (see chapter 3). As you browse through seed catalogs, select a few flowers from each of the following categories: focal-point flowers, accent flowers, filler materials, line materials, foliage (or foliage substitutes), and seed heads. Keep in mind that some plants

Bold and beautiful, focal-point flowers, such as dahlias, cardoons, sunflowers, and asters, are the center of attention.

Delicate filler materials soften dried arrangements. They include baby's breath, lady's mantle, sea lavender, German statice, and bishop's weed.

Dried-flower arrangements come alive with foliage, such as Oregon grape, scotch broom, holly, salal, and eucalyptus.

Focal-Point Flowers

Sunflowers
Asters
Roses
Lilies
Cardoons
Dahlias
Lilacs

Accent Flowers

Statice
Safflower
Ageratum
Hellebore
Marigolds
Amnobium
Small zinnias

have more than one use; for example, oregano can be used as an airy filler material but its deep purple color also makes it a wonderful accent flower.

Focal-point flowers Focal-point flowers are usually large and bold—they command attention (see the bottom photo on p. 11). As a group, focal-point flowers comprise the main characters of your arrangement. Because of their visual weight, they are generally centered over the container rather than placed at the outer edges of the design. Focal-point flowers for large arrangements may include sunflowers, dahlias, cardoons, and asters. In smaller arrangements they may be roses, daffodils, or tulips. While flowers are usually the main focus of an arrangement, other possibilities include ornamental gourds, Indian corn, or large seed heads. The arrangement on pp. 146-149 combines accessories and a flower to create the focal point.

Accent flowers If focal-point flowers are the main characters in an arrangement, then accent flowers occupy the supporting roles. They are smaller than focal-point flowers, yet they are essential for adding color, texture, and form. They harmonize with the focal-point flowers and line materials to create

pleasing, balanced designs. Examples of accent flowers include statice, safflower, flossflower, and small zinnias. Dahlias and marigolds make wonderful accent flowers in the arrangement on pp. 124-127. Their colors and shapes complement the focal-point pumpkins.

Filler materials Filler materials add a soft, airy feel to arrangements (see the top photo above). They are usually sprays of small clustered flowers, such as baby's breath, German statice, and lady's mantle, that help fill in spaces between larger blooms. Because they have a romantic, softening effect, they are not suitable for every arrangement, especially contemporary designs with clean lines. Baby's breath was used as a light and airy filler material throughout the wreath on pp. 150-153.

Line materials Line materials lend height and structure to arrangements. They radiate from the center of an arrangement (sometimes off-center in asymmetrical designs) and define the outermost points. Create pleasing rhythms in your arrangements by repeating the same line materials in graduated positions. Examples of line materials include flower spikes (liatris); foliage (eucalyptus); seed heads (ornamental grasses); or branches (pussy willow). Glycerin-preserved eucalyptus and scotch broom create beautiful sweeping lines in the arrangement on pp. 162-165.

Foliage Foliage is generally the first item placed in a fresh arrangement. It creates a lush, leafy base for the design and helps hide the moss and floral foam (see the bottom photo on the facing page). It can also be used as line and accent material. For these reasons, it should be one of the most important ingredients in dried arrangements but is routinely left out. To enliven your arrangements with foliage, select leaves that dry easily, such as salal, eucalyptus, and magnolia, and use techniques that enhance their "fresh" look, such as silica gel drying, glycerin treatments, and colored floral sprays (see chapters 2 and 3). The garland on pp. 76-79 was created with salal foliage for a fresh-looking springtime decoration.

Foliage substitutes Green plant materials are an essential element in creating dried arrangements that

Filler Materials	Line Materials	Foliage
Bishop's weed	Larkspur	Eucalyptus
Baby's breath	Blazing star	Lamb's ears
German statice	Bells of Ireland	Holly
Lady's mantle	Eucalyptus	Boxwood
Oregano	Pussy willow	Dusty miller
Sea lavender	Ornamental grasses	Lady's mantle
Yarrow		Japanese iris
	Delphinium	

Foliage substitutes, including grasses, amaranth, and safflower, offer a bit of greenery to leafless arrangements.

Seed heads contribute interesting colors and textures to arrangements. Shown here (clockwise from top): love-in-a-mist 'Transformer', ornamental grasses, starflower, poppy pods, love-in-a-mist, and orach.

Foliage Substitutes

Money plant
Safflower buds
Ornamental grasses
Love-in-a-mist
Green amaranth
Bells of Ireland
Hellebore
Hops
Fibigia

Seed Heads and Seed Pods

Love-in-a-mist
Poppy
Starflower
Grasses
Orach
Bells of Ireland
Chinese lantern

look "fresh." Unfortunately, many of the trees and shrubs that provide dried foliage take years to establish. If your dried-flower garden is in its infancy and you find yourself leafless, consider using some foliage substitutes like ornamental grasses and hops to give your designs a bit of greenery (see the photo on p. 13).

Seed heads and seed pods Seed heads are an important ingredient in dried arrangements but are not limited to one particular category (see the photo above). For instance, grasses are used as line materials while poppy pods and Chinese lanterns tuck in nicely as accents. Seed heads enhance designs by adding texture, form, and animation (in the case of some ornamental grasses). Although they are often associated with fall arrangements, they are perfectly suited for any seasonal display. For example, use delicate love-in-a-mist pods in spring arrangements; the arching stems of red switch grass in summer; bright orange Chinese lanterns in the fall; and red-tinged orach for winter-

holiday centerpieces. The topiary on pp. 132-135 highlights a wide variety of seed pod shapes, colors, and textures.

PLANNING YOUR GARDEN

Once you've chosen the various plant materials to grow and use in your arrangements, it's time to pick a garden style. The amount of dried materials you plan to grow and the size of your growing area will help determine the best garden design for your situation. Careful planning during the winter will help ensure a successful dried-flower garden in the summer.

Garden styles

There are three ways to incorporate flowers for drying in your garden: You can intersperse them in your existing landscape; grow them in crop rows; or create a cutting garden. Whichever style you choose, keep in mind that most flowers suitable for drying prefer full sun. If you are creating a new garden, choose a sunny site in your yard that is fairly level and free of large roots and rocks.

Adding to an existing landscape If you're new to dried flowers, it may be practical to incorporate them into an existing landscape. Your investment of time, money, and space are kept to a minimum, and you'll be supplied with enough material for several arrangements. Perennial borders are the perfect location for tucking in a few new plants. Choose annual and perennial dried flowers that match your present color scheme, and position them among the plants already in your border (be mindful of height considerations). An inventory of your present flowerbeds, trees, and shrubs may reveal several candidates suitable for drying (see the photo on the facing page).

In addition to your flower beds, try growing a few dried flowers in other areas of your landscape. For example, grow an assortment of dried flowers and foliage in containers on your deck or patio. Bulbs grow well in pots, as do boxwood, snapdragons, and small dahlia varieties. Your vegetable garden may also provide possibilities—oregano, dill, sage, cardoons, and ornamental peppers all dry easily. Even our small, half-barrel water garden offers cattails for fall displays.

Crop rows Crop rows are an efficient way to grow dried flowers (see the top photo on p. 16). They are an excellent choice if you plan to grow large quantities of flowers for a home-based business or to give as gifts. Even though crop rows exhibit more function than form, their straight rows make garden maintenance and harvesting a breeze.

We mulch our crop rows with 3-ft.-wide, 1mm black plastic to suppress weeds, warm the soil, and retain moisture. We use a serrated kitchen knife to cut small slits in the plastic through which we plant the seedlings. If we have a large area in production, we install a drip irrigation system, otherwise, we hand-water the rows by placing a hose nozzle over the slits. Come harvest time the wide paths easily accommodate the width of a wheelbarrow or garden cart.

On a small scale, crop rows can be incorporated into a cutting garden. Rows are well suited for growing crops that require staking, such as bishop's weed and larkspur, because the plants can be staked as a group rather than individually (see staking on p. 27).

Cutting garden If you prefer an aesthetic garden design rather than straight crop rows, consider a cutting garden. All the plants in a cutting garden are grown specifically for flower arranging (as opposed to a general diversified landscape), but they are positioned to create a pleasing garden design. A cutting

Your existing landscape may offer dried-flower possibilities. Here, blue Veronica grows among sprays of yellow lady's mantle.

To grow large amounts of dried flowers efficiently, plant them in crop rows.

Cutting gardens look charming and produce an amazing amount of flowers.

garden can be a small flower bed border or it can encompass your entire backyard.

Our small cutting garden reminds us of an old-fashioned cottage garden. Enclosed in a green picket fence, the beds overflow with a mixture of annuals, perennials, and bulbs. Although the garden is small, we managed to squeeze in a compost bin, a small tool shed, and a garden bench (see the photo below).

As shown in the garden plan on the facing page, we kept the paths narrow for maximum growing space. The rectangular beds host a wide assortment of flowers in a rainbow of colors. Some beds are reserved exclusively for annuals, which allows us to change their design every year. Even though the square footage is small, our cutting garden produces an abundance of vibrant plant materials.

Drawing a garden plan

Of the three garden styles, cutting gardens require the most planning. So developing a garden plan is the first step in creating a productive and visually pleasing cutting garden. To draw a simple garden design on graph paper, begin by measuring the perimeter of your new garden area. Assign a measurement for each graph-paper square (for example,

ANNUALS

Broomcorn
Amaranth
Starflower
Ornamental grasses
Love-in-a-mist
Zinnias
Dahlias
Sunflowers
Orach
Celosia
Statice
Bishop's weed

ANNUALS

Dahlias
Safflower
Craspedia
Bells of Ireland
Marigolds
Fibigia
Ornamental grasses
Montbretia

PERENNIALS

Delphinium

ANNUALS

Larkspur

**ANNUALS/
PERENNIALS**

Hollyhocks
Delphinium
Liatris
Poppies
Echinacia
Peony
Anenomes
Dahlias
Lady's mantle
Rose bush
Sea lavender
Echinops

**ANNUALS/
PERENNIALS**

Dahlias
Salvia
*Ornamental
  peppers*
Pansies
Dusty miller
Liatris

PERENNIALS

*Climbing
  roses (arbor)*
Lilac
Gladwin iris
Hellebores

This is a plan of our 32-ft. x 32-ft. dried-flower garden.

Use a graph-paper grid to determine the position and spacing of the plants in your garden. This is an example of a 3-ft. x 10-ft. dried-flower border that contains a good selection of plant types for flower arranging, including focal point and accent flowers, line materials, and foliage substitutes.

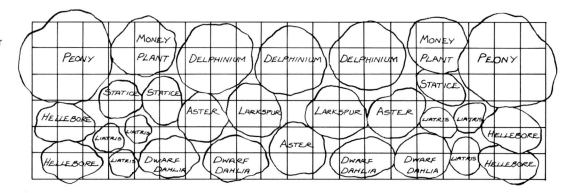

I square equals 6 in.). With a pencil, draw your garden's perimeter lines to scale, then determine the width of your paths and the size of your garden beds. If you want to include garden accessories such as a bench, birdbath, or compost bin, incorporate their dimensions into your plan. Rework your graph-paper sketch until the final layout is a functional yet pleasing design.

Next, organize the list of plants you'll be growing by color, height, shape, and type (perennial, annual, etc.). Draw circles on your graph paper indicating the placement of each plant and be mindful of the spacing requirements (see the drawing above). As you design, create pleasing combinations by visualizing how the colors, heights, and shapes will interact with one another.

GROWING PLANTS FROM SEED

Now that you've designed your new garden, it's time to transform your graph-paper plan into reality. The first step along that path is starting your plants from seed. Over the years, we've grown thousands of

plants for our dried-flower business. Yet every spring we wait with excited anticipation for the first seeds to germinate. To watch a minute seed transform into a tall plant is truly an amazing process. With a few basic tools and a little bit of time, it's possible to grow enough plants to fill your entire garden.

Where to start your seeds

We suggest you start your seeds indoors in flats or containers (see the photos on the facing page). Unfortunately, seeds sown directly into the garden often germinate erratically due to fluctuations in soil temperature and moisture. Mice, birds, and slugs add to the problem by dining on seeds and newly germinated seedlings. Finally, weeds will germinate simultaneously with your flower seeds, making it difficult to differentiate between the two. Although starting seeds indoors takes extra time, your reward is healthy, robust seedlings that are ready for planting in your freshly tilled garden.

The number of plants you plan to grow will determine where you start your seeds indoors. A

bright windowsill is perfect for starting a small number of seedlings (for example, enough to fill several patio containers). But if you're growing several flats to fill an entire garden, you'll need to set up your growing area in a larger space.

The growing area should be warm and receive plenty of light, such as a windowsill, spare bedroom, or backyard greenhouse. With a few adjustments, an insulated garage or basement (that remains well above freezing) works just as well. These otherwise cool, dark rooms make wonderful propagation areas if you provide artificial illumination and bottom heat (see p. 21).

Propagating plants from seed

Once you've decided where to start your seedlings indoors, you will need a few basic supplies: containers, growing medium, seeds, labels, grow lights, electric heating cables (optional), a watering can, and a cold frame. In the following pages we will discuss these supplies in detail and the simple steps to starting your own dried-flower plants from seed.

Before you begin Seeds can be started in a variety of containers, including paper cups, egg cartons, plastic flats, and recycled nursery pots. Make sure there are adequate drainage holes in the containers you choose. We start our seeds in 11-in. by 21-in. plastic trays.

Successful plant propagation begins with proper hygiene. If you're reusing pots or flats from previous years, they need to be sterilized in a 10% bleach solution. Mix the solution in a deep laundry sink or clean plastic garbage can, and soak the containers for several minutes. Once the containers are sterilized, rinse them with clean water.

Without sterilization, water- and soil-borne fungi can cause a plant disease called damping-off. It strikes young seedlings, withering their roots and stems. Use the following tips to further discourage damping-off:

- Have good air circulation in your growing area.
- Sow your seeds thinly.
- Don't overwater.
- Use a sterilized growing medium.

Left: With a few simple tools and supplies, you can grow most of your dried flowers from seed.

Above: Start your seedlings indoors. Protect your work surfaces with plastic sheeting and supply supplemental light.

Use a sterile, soilless mix to fill your seed trays. It drains freely yet retains moisture.

For optimum germination, use fresh seeds and lightly sprinkle them on the soil surface.

We use a sterile, commercially made soilless potting mix (see the photo at left). Soilless growing mediums are usually composed of several ingredients, including peat moss, vermiculite, perlite, sand, and nutrients. They often vary in texture and nutrients, so make sure the one you choose is formulated for starting seeds.

Fill the sterilized containers with a soilless mix, then rap the container on a tabletop to settle the medium. Continue filling the containers until the medium reaches just below the rim. We premoisten the soilless mix before filling our trays.

Sowing seeds For optimum germination rates, buy fresh seeds each year and keep them stored in a cool, dry, well-ventilated location. Many seeds require preplanting treatments to break their dormancy. It's important to read the growing information on each seed packet several weeks before you plant (also, refer to the growing instructions in the Plant Guide, beginning on p. 170). Treatments may include:

- prechilling the seeds in a refrigerator (stratification)
- presoaking to soften hard seed coats
- chipping or nicking hard seed coats with a utility knife to increase moisture absorption (scarification)

Some seeds require light for germination. Sow these seeds on the surface of the soilless mix and do not cover them with additional growing medium. (This method is known as surface-sowing.)

When you're ready to plant, lightly scatter your seeds onto the soilless mix and cover them with additional medium if they don't require light for germination (see the bottom photo on the facing page). If you are planting large seeds, such as cardoons or sunflowers, plant the individual seeds in 3-in. to 4-in. pots.

Water the newly seeded flats with either a watering can or a fog nozzle, as shown in the photo at right. Use a watering can to water flats containing medium- and large-size seeds. Flats containing small or surface-sown seeds should be watered with a fog nozzle or a watering can equipped with a fine rose. Careful, light watering will prevent these seeds from being displaced or covered by too much soilless mix.

Each flat will need a plant tag. When the plants are transplanted to the garden, their tags go with them. We use sturdy white plastic labels to record a variety of information including the plant's name, seed supplier, color, planting date, and germination date. If a plant performs particularly well during the season, we use the information to grow it again the following year.

Germination Most seeds germinate quickly in warm soil. While many seeds can be started at room temperature, gentle bottom heat (68°F to 86°F) from propagation heating cables or mats will speed germination (carefully follow the manufacturer's instructions for using these devices). Be aware that heating cables can quickly dry out the soilless mix in a flat so you may need to water often. Once the seeds germinate, they will no longer need bottom heat, but you should continue to keep the flats in a warm, bright area.

The young seedlings will require approximately 16 hours of light a day to prevent weak and leggy stems. Supplement the natural light in your growing area with grow lamps or fluorescent lights (if you

Cover the seeds with additional growing medium (according to label instructions) and water them in.

use a fluorescent shoplight fixture, equip it with one cool and one warm fluorescent tube to produce the broadest spectrum of light). Even if your indoor growing area is near a bright window, seedlings will benefit from supplemental light. Hang the fixtures so the lights are 6 in. to 8 in. above the foliage.

Transplanting (pricking-out) When the seedlings are large enough to handle, transplant them to cell flats filled with moist, soilless mix. We use 11-in. by 21-in. plastic cell flats containing 72 cells each, or small nursery packs containing 6 cells, as shown in the photo on p. 22. (Most of our seedlings remain in the cell flats until we plant them in the garden.)

Use the point of a pencil or a small metal skewer to gently loosen the soilless mix and lift the individual seedlings from their tray—be careful not to break their roots. Always handle fragile seedlings by their leaves, not their stems. Make a hole in the mix

When the seedlings are large enough to handle, transplant them to individual cell flats or packs.

of each individual cell, then carefully lower the root of each seedling into the hole. Gently press the mix around each stem. Water the seedlings with a watering can or a fog nozzle to settle the mix around the roots. To allow time for the newly transplanted seedlings to become established, keep the flats in a bright location at room temperature for several days.

CARING FOR SEEDLINGS

As you transplant your seedlings into cell flats, your indoor growing area will become increasingly crowded. Alleviate the congestion by moving the flats to an outdoor growing area. With a bit of care and nurturing, the tiny seedlings will quickly grow

into vigorous young plants. Once the weather moderates, complete the final step of hardening-off your seedlings in preparation for planting them in your garden.

Using a cold frame

Unless you live in a warm climate, you will need a cold frame to successfully grow seedlings. It can be a permanent structure made from wood and glass or a temporary cloche made from a series of wire hoops and plastic sheeting. If you plan to grow your own seedlings every year, we recommend building a permanent cold frame. The wisdom of that decision will be evident during the first spring windstorm.

Within a few days of transplanting the tiny sprouts into cell flats, move them to your cold frame. This will adapt the seedlings to outdoor temperatures without exposing them to inclement weather. Begin the acclimation process by leaving the flats in the cold frame during the day, but bring them indoors at night. After several days, they can be left in the cold frame 24 hours as long as the outdoor temperature stays above freezing.

Check your cold frame twice a day. Each morning, open the cold frame lid about 8 in. for adequate air circulation. If the sun is shining, even in cool weather, the high temperature inside a closed cold frame can damage small seedlings (in cold, stormy weather, leave the cold frame closed). Before dusk, close the frame to preserve as much heat as possible for the night.

On cold nights that dip to near freezing, there are several ways to keep your seedlings warm. The simplest solution is to bring the flats indoors; however, this may be impractical if you're growing a large number of seedlings. Instead, leave the flats in the cold frame and use chicken brooder lamps (available at most farm and feed stores) equipped with standard 100-watt bulbs to warm the inside air temperature. In each of our cold frames, we hang twin lamps 12 in. to 18 in. above the foliage (see the photo below). Bring tender annuals, such as ornamental peppers, indoors on these exceedingly cold nights. For extra protection, insulate the cold frame by covering it with old blankets. Remove the coverings in the morning.

The soil moisture in each flat must be monitored as closely as the air temperature. Individual cells dry out quickly and may need watering once or twice a day (especially in hot, sunny weather). Frequent watering leaches nutrients from the soilless mix. To counteract this, begin fertilizing your seedlings with an all-purpose, water-soluble fertilizer when they are about two weeks old. Follow the instructions on the label, but dilute the solution to half-strength.

As the seedlings grow, open your cold frame completely on mild days. The cool breezes will produce

Grow your seedlings in a cold frame. On cold nights, increase the inside air temperature with standard light bulbs.

stocky seedlings with strong stems. Also, air circulation reduces the risk of damping-off, a potential problem in warm, humid cold frames.

Hardening-off seedlings

As the days become warmer and planting is but a week or two away, it's time to harden off your seedlings. This is the process of slowly acclimating them to outdoor conditions until they are no longer dependent on the cold frame for protection.

About 10 days before you plant your seedlings in the garden, start leaving the cold frame completely open during the day and gradually increase the amount it is open at night. As a precaution, close the lid if nighttime temperatures approach freezing.

If your planting date is delayed due to inclement weather or your plants grow faster than expected, the seedlings may become root-bound. To determine if this is a problem, gently remove a sampling of seedlings from their cell flats. They are root-bound if you see more roots than soil. If only a few are root-bound, transplant them to slightly larger containers and continue growing them in your cold frame. However, if most of your plants are root-bound, it's best to transplant them to the garden. Protect them under temporary cloches until the weather moderates. While most seedlings can tolerate crowded roots for short periods of time, the growth of some plants, such as larkspur and nigella, will be stunted if they are root-bound for too long.

INTO THE GARDEN

While your seedlings are gaining strength in the cold frame, turn your attention to preparing their final home in the garden. If you're creating a new garden, begin working the soil as soon as it is friable and the weather allows. When the site is ready, the seedlings are grown, and the weather moderates, all your hard work and planning will come to fruition on planting day!

Site preparation

The first step in creating a new garden site is to remove any existing sod. Once the soil is free of grass, stones, and debris, refer to your graph paper garden design (see p. 18) to lay out the beds and paths. Use a measuring tape and the measurements from your plan to locate the perimeter lines of each bed. Pound in a stake at each corner, then run strings to define the borders (see the photo on the facing page). With a square-bladed spade, dig the perimeter edges using the strings as a guide.

Deeply cultivate the soil with either a tiller or a shovel. Once all the large clods are reduced to small crumbles, amend the soil with organic matter. We add peat moss, compost, and processed chicken manure. Most dried-flower species will grow in average garden soil, but amendments lighten the soil, increase moisture retention, and provide nutrients—all of which encourage plant growth. Our soil tends to be acidic, so we test the pH and add lime if necessary.

With all the amendments sprinkled on the soil surface, use a spading fork to incorporate them deep into the root zone. Once you rake the beds smooth and remove the stakes and strings, your garden is ready for planting. During the growing season, we apply a top dressing of an all-purpose, time-released fertilizer (following the label directions) around any plants that look peaked.

If you are creating a small crop-row garden, use the same method just described. However, if you are growing a large production area, it's best to till the soil, lay down the plastic mulch in rows, and fertilize as you water during the summer with a water-soluble fertilizer. In the fall, plant a cover crop over the area and till it under the following spring to increase organic matter in the soil.

If you are incorporating plants into an existing landscape, dig individual holes for the new plants and amend the back-fill soil with compost and peat moss. During the growing season, top-dress the area with an all-purpose, time-released fertilizer.

Planting out seedlings

When your garden is fully prepared and the temperature no longer dips below freezing, it's time to plant. Choose a mild, overcast day to avoid stressing the young seedlings. Before you begin, water the flats thoroughly and let them drain.

Lay out your garden design on the soil surface with stakes and string. Then deeply cultivate and amend the soil.

To remove the seedlings from their trays, squeeze the diagonal corners of each cell on the bottom of the flat, then gently lift the plants out by their leaves. With two fingers, make a small hole in the garden soil and place the root ball in the depression. Firm the soil around the roots and thoroughly water them in.

Mulching your garden is the final step in the planting process. Applying a 2-in. to 3-in. layer of mulch over the entire garden will prevent most weed seeds from germinating. The few that do sprout are easily pulled from the mulch. Keep an inch or two of air space around the newly planted seedlings—the mulch can be drawn closer to the stems as the plants grow taller. We use peat moss on the beds and bark chips on the paths (see the photo on the facing page). Other organic mulches suitable for garden beds include grass clippings, chopped leaves,

After weeks of growing seedlings and preparing garden beds, it's exciting to finally combine the two.

and compost. Mulch the paths with durable materials such as sawdust, nut hulls, or straw to withstand foot traffic.

In early spring, we continue to protect tender annuals against unexpected cold snaps. Glass cloches work well and look charming, but inverted nursery pots or plastic sheeting secured to wire hoops keep the plants just as warm on cold nights.

GARDEN MAINTENANCE

After all your careful preparations and nurturing of small seedlings, take a moment to enjoy your completed garden. Time's up! Unfortunately, a gardener's work is never done. To keep the plants thriving and the garden looking neat and tidy, routine maintenance such as watering, weeding, and pest control must be done throughout the summer months.

Watering

Water is an essential ingredient of a lush, productive garden. Even though the amendments and mulches you applied in the spring will increase the soil's moisture retention, routine watering is still necessary throughout the growing season. Early morning is the best time to water. If you wait until evening, your plants will remain wet through the night, increasing the risk of fungus and mildew. In the afternoon, much of the water is wasted to evaporation.

How much to water depends on the weather, soil, and the plant varieties you grow. During hot, dry, or windy weather, check the soil regularly. Avoid frequent, light waterings. Instead, thoroughly soak your garden to encourage the roots to grow deep into the soil where there is less chance of them drying out

Mulch suppresses weeds and retains soil moisture. We use bark chips on our paths and peat moss on the beds. Glass cloches protect our ornamental peppers in early spring.

between waterings. Porous, sandy soil will need watering more frequently than clay soils. However, both will benefit from the addition of organic matter. If you live in an area where water use is restricted, consider growing a greater number of drought-tolerant plants, such as yarrow, gomphrena, baby's breath, and gladwin iris.

There are a variety of ways to water a garden. When our plants are small, we use the efficiency of an overhead sprinkler. When they begin to bloom, we switch to a hand-held watering nozzle, as shown in the top photo on p. 28. Hand watering keeps water off the foliage and flowers. This reduces the risk of fungus and keeps the flowers in perfect condition. Also, it prevents tall plants from toppling under the weight of the water. Soaker hoses are another excellent way to water your garden without wetting the flowers and foliage.

Weeding and deadheading

Early in our gardening careers we came to the realization that there was one more certainty in life besides death and taxes—weeds! Mulching is your best defense against weeds (it does nothing for death and taxes!). Even if a few renegades pop through, they are easily pulled. Remove them while they're young. Deeply rooted, mature weeds are difficult to pull and will compete with your flowers for sunlight and nutrients. Of course, the best way to reduce weeding is to never let a weed go to seed.

As you pull weeds and tidy up your garden, take time to deadhead your plants, unless you're growing them for their seed pods. Plucking off spent flowers keeps your garden looking clean and orderly and encourages the growth of side shoots and more blooms (see the bottom photo on p. 28).

Staking

While most dried flowers don't require staking, it's essential for some, especially in windy weather. Dahlias, for instance, produce strong, upright stems, but the weight of their blooms tends to topple them. To prevent this, insert a support stake as you plant each tuberous root or clump. If you wait until the plants have grown, you risk damaging the roots as you pound in the stakes.

Hand-water to keep moisture off the blooms.

Deadheading keeps the garden looking tidy and the plants blooming profusely.

It's impractical to stake individual plants if you plan to grow a lot of one species, such as larkspur or bishop's weed. Instead, grow them in rows and support them as a group. Pound in 3-ft. stakes, spaced 3 ft. apart, around the perimeter of the row. Run string from stake to stake about 20 in. from the ground. Then run strings down the center of the row in a crisscross pattern (see the bottom photo on p. 16). The plants will grow up through the crisscross pattern, supported by the strings and each other.

Controlling pests and diseases

Insects and diseases have been an annoyance in our dried-flower gardens but not an insurmountable problem. We use organic methods of control whenever possible and try to prevent infestations before they begin.

Removing weeds and debris increases air circulation among the plants and helps to prevent diseases from taking hold. Watering in the morning minimizes the damp conditions that encourage fungi and bacteria. To further prevent infestations, do a thorough fall cleanup and burn any infected plant material.

Insect pests, such as the cucumber beetles shown in the photo at right, enjoy dining on soft-petaled flowers. To combat these and other insects, start with the least invasive methods of eradication and increase your defenses as necessary. For example, we hand-pick cucumber beetles off the blooms as we make the daily rounds of our garden. Aphids can often be dislodged with a good spray of water from a garden hose.

Most of the species we grow are profuse bloomers, providing enough flowers for arrangements as well as a few for the bugs. However, if insects become a persistent problem on your plants, you may need to resort to insecticidal soaps and plant-derived insecticides such as pyrethrum and rotenone. These types of insecticides kill the beneficial insects along with the pests, though, so be sure to carefully follow the instructions on the label.

Control pests, such as these cucumber beetles, before they devour all your hard work.

GENERAL HARVESTING TECHNIQUES

By mid to late summer, your garden will overflow with flowers. Most likely, there will be an abundance to dry as well as plenty for fresh flower arrangements. Although this is the busiest time of year, there is usually something to harvest from early spring through late fall. Depending on where you live, it may be possible to harvest year-round. This is especially true if you supplement your garden harvest with plant materials collected from the wild, such as cones, branches, and seed heads. Whether you harvest from your garden or from nature, use the following harvesting techniques to help produce quality dried materials (refer to the

We harvest into baskets. The cane basket holds four small water glasses to keep the flowers fresh for silica drying.

Plant Guide, beginning on p. 170, for specific harvesting instructions).

Before you begin to harvest, allow time for any morning dew or raindrops to completely evaporate. Plant materials harboring excess moisture have a greater chance of mildewing. Pick materials that are in prime condition. Petals with brown spots or bug-eaten edges look worse after drying. Also, check your garden daily—a flower may be in bud one day and in full bloom the next.

The most important tool for harvesting flowers is a good pair of hand shears or clippers. We use needle-nose clippers (also called grape shears) because their slender, tapered blades easily maneuver among cluttered stems. Their vinyl-coated handles reduce the chance of blisters, while the spring action minimizes hand fatigue. Although household scissors are less expensive, they can cause blisters and have difficulty cutting through tough or woody stems.

In addition to a good pair of shears, you will need harvesting baskets and containers. For plant materials destined for silica gel, bring along a container of water. These materials need to be kept fresh until the moment you place them in the desiccant. To prevent them from wilting, cut the stems long and place them in water as you harvest. Keep all cut materials out of direct sunlight.

Use a basket, cardboard box, or wheelbarrow to carry freshly harvested plants for air-drying. Even though the plants eventually wilt during the drying process, try to keep them as fresh as possible until you hang them to dry. Always keep them out of the hot sun as you bundle. We lay several sheets of newspaper over our harvesting baskets and then bundle the flowers under a shady tree.

As you bundle, sort your freshly cut flowers by color. This saves time during the assembly of your dried-flower arrangements. The delicate blooms may shatter if you try to extract just a few stems from a dried bundle of mixed colors.

During the hot days of summer, sort and bundle your flowers in the shade to keep them fresh.

COLLECTING FROM THE WILD

Wood lots, roadsides, swamps, and the seashore can offer interesting dried materials. The selection includes cones, grasses, branches, cattails, and driftwood. Before you harvest in the wild, consult your local county extension agent regarding endangered species. Also, if you don't own the land, obtain permission from the property owner before you pick. Minimize the impact to the ecosystem by leaving plenty of flowers and seed heads behind.

Every area of the country has unique indigenous plants that can be incorporated into dried arrangements. At right is a list of plant materials that we gather in western Washington. Take a walk in your own woodlands and see what you can find.

Teasel	Cones
Scotch broom	Seed pods
Queen Anne's lace	Branches and twigs
Salal	Pussywillow branches
Oregon grape	Cattails
Grasses	
Horsetail	

Chapter 2

Drying Techniques

Preserve the colors and textures of your summer garden using a variety of flower-drying techniques. Time and patience are the only other prerequisites for capturing the essence of your landscape.

Air-
Drying

Drying
Rack

Silica Gel

Glycerin

B y midsummer your garden will be in full bloom and offering

something new to harvest each day. Before the harvest begins, determine

where you will dry and preserve this abundance of plant material.

   Although dried materials never look quite as resplendent as fresh, they can

come close if you choose the best drying method for each plant. This chapter

outlines three basic methods of drying and preserving flowers, foliage, and

seed pods: air-drying, drying with silica gel, and preserving with glycerin (for

drying instructions on specific plants, refer to the Plant Guide beginning on

p. 170). We've also included some tips on how to store your plant materials

once they are preserved and dried.

During the summer, air-dry plant materials in a backyard drying shed. In the spring, convert it into a greenhouse for starting seedlings.

If you grow just a few flowers, consider using a closet to dry and store your plant materials.

AIR-DRYING

The easiest, least expensive, and most common method of preserving flowers is air-drying. Air-drying techniques include hanging flower bundles upside down; standing plant materials upright in empty buckets or containers; and placing foliage or flower heads flat on drying racks. It usually takes between 3 days and 3 weeks to air-dry plant materials. The amount of time fluctuates with variances in air temperature, humidity, stem thickness, bundle size, and plant species. For instance, thick cardoon stems take longer to dry than the delicate stems of baby's breath.

For the best results, choose a location that is dry, warm, dark, and well ventilated. Suitable areas inside your home include an attic, closet, or spare bedroom. Other possibilities include a loft in a garage, storage building, or barn, although there may be a greater risk of insect and rodent damage in these locations (see p. 45). Plant materials dried in uninsulated areas must be brought indoors and stored properly before the first fall rains because humid conditions may encourage mildew.

If you are short on space, consider building a small, backyard drying shed like the one shown in the right photo on the facing page. You can either build a simple 2x4 frame (as we did) or purchase a kit for making a small greenhouse frame (see Sources on p. 207) and cover it with 6mm black plastic. In the summer, the black plastic covering on the shed absorbs the sun's radiation and heats the shed's interior for fast drying. Most flowers that are dried quickly at high temperatures (100°F to 125°F) maintain their colors and are less likely to mildew during the drying process. Each spring, change the black plastic to clear plastic and use the structure as a greenhouse for starting seedlings.

Hang-drying

Hang-drying is the easiest method of air-drying plant materials. The process consists of gathering several stems together and securing them with a rubber band (explained at right). This bundle is then hung upside down to dry.

Prepare your drying area by stretching lines of wire from wall to wall or across ceiling rafters. We install screw eyes on opposite wall studs and stretch 17-gauge fencing wire between them. Once the wires are in place, hang the flower bundles by spreading them in half and slipping them over the lines (see the left photo on p. 38). If you plan to dry just a few flowers in a closet, use coat hangers and paper clips to hang your bundles. Start by bending a paper clip into an S-shape hook. Slip one end of the paper clip onto the bundle's rubber band and twist the other end onto a coat hanger (see the left photo on the facing page).

BUNDLING STEMS FOR HANG-DRYING

We use rubber bands to hold our flower bunches together. Unlike twist-ties or string, rubber bands hold the bundles securely as the stems dry and shrink. If you are bundling a lot of flowers, this fast and easy method of banding will save time.

1. Hold your flower bundle in the middle with one hand and hook a rubber band over 2 or 3 sturdy stems with the other. Slide the rubber band up the stems until it is close to the hand holding the flowers.

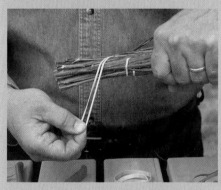

2. Stretch the rubber band taut as you wind it around the stems several times, moving toward the cut end of the stems.

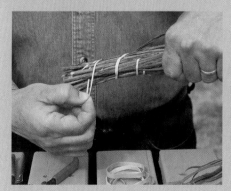

3. Hook the rubber band around any 2 or 3 sturdy stems.

Whether you suspend your plant materials from wires or coat hangers, make sure the bundles hang perpendicular to the ground to avoid curved stems. Also, be aware that nigella and poppy pods release thousands of seeds during the drying process. For easy cleanup, spread newspaper on the floor below these pods.

Most seed pods hang-dry easily and hold their shapes well. The same is true of many flowers, especially those with small flower heads (baby's breath, lady's mantle) or stiff bracts (straw flowers, gomphrena, ammobium, knapweed, cardoon, oregano, hops). Flowers with soft, broad petals, such as roses and peonies, can be hang-dried, although they shrivel considerably. We suggest you dry these flower types in silica gel. Stiff, leathery foliage, including magnolia, salal, and holly, are also good candidates for hang-drying. To prevent excessive curling, hang-dry them at room temperature (also see Flat-drying on the facing page).

Upright-drying

Some flowers dry easily standing upright in empty containers or buckets. The wired flower heads of sea holly and strawflowers, for instance, can be placed in canning jars or coffee cans to dry. If drying space is limited on your hanging lines, consider drying stiff-stemmed plant materials, such as broomcorn, money plant, teasel, and cattails, upright in buckets.

Upright-drying serves an additional purpose besides saving space. When plants are hung upside down, the pull of gravity produces very straight

Separate flower bundles in half to hang them over wire lines.

Dry wired flower heads and plant materials with stiff stems upright in containers.

stems as the plants dry. Arrangements created entirely with straight stems may look stiff and contrived. But plants dried upright (especially ornamental grasses) achieve graceful arching stems under the influence of gravity and will add variety to any arrangement.

Flat-drying

The final method of air-drying is to place plant materials flat on a drying rack. The drying racks shown here have a different purpose. The table drying rack (topped with chicken wire) allows you to air-dry flowers in an upright position with their stems attached (see the photo at right). The rack is used for flowers that would otherwise curl closed if they were dried upside down, such as Queen Anne's lace

A table drying rack like the one shown above is easy to construct and perfect for air-drying flowers such as marigolds and Queen Anne's lace.

Air-dry foliage and small flower heads on a window-screen drying rack like the one shown at left.

and marigolds. The wire supports the flower heads while the stems hang straight below. For added support to the petals, you can place a single layer of newspaper or kraft paper over the wire and use scissors to poke holes for the stems to hang through.

The window-screen drying rack is used for individual leaves and small flowers that don't have stems attached. The tight mesh of the screen supports the material yet allows air circulation (see the bottom photo on p. 39). Dry the leaves of lamb's ears, dusty miller, lady's mantle, and Japanese iris by placing them individually on the screens. Gently press them beneath the weight of a newspaper section to prevent them from curling. Air-dry small flower heads, such as rose buds, globe amaranth, or botanical ingredients for potpourri, by scattering the blooms evenly across the screens.

If you must harvest when the flowers are wet, allow time for water to evaporate completely before placing your plant material in silica gel. Place the flowers in a vase of water overnight, and by the next day they should be ready for the drying process.

DESICCANTS

The ultimate goal of flower preservation is to create dried flowers that look almost as fresh as they did the day you harvested them. While that level of perfection is not attainable, flowers dried in desiccants come close. Flowers that would otherwise shrivel during air-drying hold their natural shapes when dried in desiccants. A variety of inexpensive desiccants are readily available including sand and a mixture of borax and cornmeal.

None, however, work as well as silica gel crystals (which look similar to pure white sand), available at most craft stores. Although it is more expensive than the other drying agents, it's well worth the investment. It can be reused for years and the resulting dried flowers are spectacular. We've had wonderful results drying peonies, sunflowers, lilacs, zinnias, lilies, hyacinths, and daffodils to name a few. Fern fronds and other delicate foliage also dry well in silica gel. If you are uncertain about which drying method to use (silica gel, air-drying, or glycerin), silica gel will usually produce the best results for most plant materials.

Traditional drying with silica gel

Drying plant materials in silica gel is a simple process resulting in perfectly dried flowers and foliage in just a few days. Start by harvesting flowers in their prime (overly mature blooms may shatter once they are dry). While it's not necessary to dry only one plant species at a time, choose plant materials with similar characteristics (stem and petal thickness) so they dry at the same rate.

The plant materials must be free of surface moisture before placing them in silica gel. Do

HOW TO REUSE SILICA GEL

Silica gel can be reused for years. Most brands have special blue indicator crystals mixed in with the white. When the blue granules turn pink, it indicates the crystals have absorbed all the moisture they can hold and they will need to be dried out before their next use.

To reuse your silica gel, dry it in either a conventional or microwave oven. To use a conventional oven, pour a layer of silica gel in the bottom of an uncovered glass baking dish (you can use a metal pan, but it may rust over time). Place it in a 275°F oven for about an hour.

In a microwave, place no more than 2 pounds of silica gel in the bottom of a microwave-safe dish. Set the microwave on high for 5 minutes. Stir the granules every minute.

With either method, the silica gel is dry when the indicator crystals have returned to their bright blue color. Once the silica gel is dry and cools to room temperature, store it in a sealed plastic container. Occasionally pour the crystals through a sieve to remove leftover pieces of plant debris.

---

your harvesting in late morning or early afternoon once the dew and any raindrops have evaporated. During rainy spells, bring wet blooms and foliage indoors and stand them in vases of water, allowing them to dry overnight (see the photo on the facing page).

For this traditional method you will need:
- a plastic container with a tight lid (a plastic shoe or sweater box works well)
- silica gel (you will need at least 5 to 10 pounds)
- a ½-cup measuring scoop
- an assortment of freshly cut flowers or foliage

1. Harvest and prepare the flowers for drying. While most flowers, including peonies and hollyhocks, are removed and dried separately from their stems, some flowers, such as hyacinths and daffodils, are dried with their stems attached.
2. Pour a 1-in. layer of silica gel into an empty plastic container. Place each bloom faceup on top of the crystals (see the photo at right). Arrange them so they do not overlap or touch the sides of the container.

3. Use a ½-cup measuring scoop to gently pour silica gel over the flowers (see the top photo on p. 42). Completely bury the blooms in silica gel without compressing the petals in the process. If you pour too quickly, the petals will bend and fold under the weight of the crystals. Start by pouring the silica gel into the spaces between the flowers. As you pour, the grains will slowly infiltrate each bloom. Continue adding silica gel until the flowers are completely covered. Deep containers allow you to add a second layer of flowers on top of the first as long as you can fit ½ in. to 1 in. of silica gel between layers.
4. Secure the lid on your container. Most flowers dry in 2 to 7 days, but the length of time will vary with each type of plant. After several days, slowly pour off the top layer of silica gel and feel the flower

These freshly cut zinnias are sitting on a bed of silica gel ready to be covered. The flowers are arranged so they do not touch each other.

Slowly pour additional silica gel around and over the blooms until they are completely covered.

Once the plant materials are dry, carefully pour off the silica gel.

petals for crispness. Silica-dried flowers are fragile so check carefully. If they aren't dry, pour the silica back over the blooms, replace the lid, and wait a day or two longer.

5. Once the blooms are dry, remove them from the container (flowers that remain in silica gel too long may shatter). Slowly pour off the silica gel into a second container; if it is poured too quickly the delicate petals may break. Gently remove each bloom as it is revealed from beneath the crystals.

6. Silica-dried plant materials quickly reabsorb moisture from the air, so if you don't plan to surface-seal the flowers immediately (for more on this, see p. 59), keep them stored in a covered plastic container with a thin layer of silica gel on the bottom.

Microwave drying with silica gel

Microwave drying is basically the same technique as silica gel drying with the added element of heat. This process dries flowers quickly, which is an advantage if you have a lot of flowers to dry and a limited amount of silica gel. However, we prefer to silica-dry our flowers without a microwave for consistent results. The variances in microwave ovens, the moisture content in plant materials, and the number of flowers being dried make it difficult to give exact drying times. This process takes experimentation; record your results for future reference. Dry only one plant species at a time because each may dry at a different rate. Seed pods, buds, lilacs, and dogwood don't dry well in a microwave.

For this method you will need:

- a microwave oven
- a microwave-safe dish
- a glass of water
- silica gel
- a ½-cup measuring scoop
- freshly cut flowers or foliage

1. Pour a 1-in. layer of silica gel into the bottom of the microwave-safe dish.

2. Place the blooms faceup on the crystals. (Don't dry flowers with wired stems in a microwave.) Arrange them side-by-side so they do not overlap or touch the sides of the dish.

3. Use a ½-cup measuring scoop to gently pour silica gel over the flowers. Completely bury the blooms in silica gel without compressing the petals. If you pour too quickly, the petals will fold under the weight of the crystals. Start by pouring the silica gel into the spaces between the flowers. As you pour, the grains will slowly infiltrate each bloom. Continue adding silica gel until the flowers are completely covered. Dry only one layer of flowers or foliage at a time.

4. Place the uncovered dish in the microwave along with a glass of water. Select a medium or defrost power control setting and set the timer for 2 to 5 minutes.

5. When the time is up, take the dish out of the microwave and allow it to stand undisturbed until the silica gel is room temperature.

6. Gently pour off the silica gel and check the petals for crispness. If they are not dry, replace the silica gel and heat the dish for a minute or two longer. If they are dry, remove the plants from the dish. Slowly pour off the silica gel into a second container; if it is poured too quickly the delicate petals may break. Gently remove each bloom as it is revealed from beneath the crystals. If you don't plan to surface-seal the flowers immediately (see p. 59), keep them stored in a covered plastic container with a thin layer of silica gel on the bottom.

GLYCERIN

Preserving plant materials with glycerin is an interesting process. When freshly harvested plants are placed in a glycerin solution, they absorb the mixture systemically. When the plants are hung to dry, the water evaporates but the glycerin remains within the stems and leaves. Plant materials preserved with glycerin are pliable and easy to arrange because of their flexibility. While some flowers, including baby's breath, sea holly, and lady's mantle, can be treated with glycerin, we primarily use it for seed heads and foliage.

Some air-dried seed heads, including those of orach, starflower, and bells of Ireland, tend to shatter easily; however, when treated with glycerin, they stay firmly attached to their stems. Glycerin also improves foliage. Air-drying often produces shriveled foliage, but leaves preserved with glycerin retain their natural form. For best results choose foliage that is thick and leathery, such as salal and eucalyptus. Harvest in late summer or early autumn when the foliage is mature (immature foliage that is glycerin-treated will droop and wither). Woody stems require special preparation for better glycerin absorption. Use a knife to scrape off the bottom inch of bark and make a cross-split cut at the end of each stem.

To preserve with glycerin, you will need:

- glycerin (available at most drug stores)
- a large glass pitcher
- glass jars or vases
- freshly cut plant materials

1. Into a large pitcher, pour 1 part glycerin, then add 2 parts nearly boiling water, stir, and let cool.
2. Fill several jars or vases with 2 in. to 3 in. of the glycerin solution.
3. Remove any foliage from the lower portion of the stems and place the freshly cut material into the jars. Place jars containing tall plants, such as bells of Ireland, inside an empty 5-gallon bucket or tall cardboard box. The large outside container will support the stems and keep the jar from toppling. Limit the number of stems per jar to maintain good air circulation.
4. Keep the plant material soaking indoors and out of direct sunlight for 3 or 4 days. Check the glycerin-solution level each day and add more if necessary. Plant materials absorb at different rates depending on their size and species. For instance, woody plants may take longer than 3 or 4 days. Sufficiently treated materials feel pliable and, in the case of foliage, may darken or change color. If plant materials are left soaking too long, beads of glycerin will weep from the leaves and stems. It can be wiped off with a tissue, but we remove the treated materials before this point to avoid a sticky problem.
5. Remove the plant materials from the jars and cut off the portion of stem that was submerged in the solution. Bundle several stems together with a rubber band and hang them upside down to dry

in a warm, dark location for a week or two. The remaining glycerin solution can be reused even if it has darkened. Add a drop or two of bleach to keep the mixture fresh.

STORING DRIED FLOWERS

Once you've grown, harvested, and dried a beautiful selection of flowers, it's important to store them properly. Light, humidity, insects, and rodents cause the majority of damage to dried flowers. Use the following storage suggestions to keep your plant materials looking their best for future use.

Storage techniques

Silica-dried flowers are fragile and quickly reabsorb humidity. Before storing these flowers for a long period of time, spray them with a surface sealer (for more on this, see p. 59). After they are completely dry, place them side-by-side in a plastic container with a secure lid. Even though sealed flowers are fairly durable, we put a small, open jar of silica gel in the box for extra humidity control. Be sure to label the contents on the outside of each container and store them in a dry, dark location. If you need to temporarily store unsealed flowers, place them in a covered plastic container with a thin layer of silica gel on the bottom (see the photo on the facing page).

Store glycerin-preserved and air-dried plant materials the same way. However, they must be placed in separate boxes because the moisture from glycerin-treated plants can damage air-dried flowers. Wrap individual flower bundles (either air-dried or glycerin-preserved) in newspaper or kraft paper, and lay them on their sides in a cardboard box. If the

Maintain the quality of your dried plant materials by carefully storing them for future use. Use cardboard boxes to store air-dried and glycerin-preserved materials, and plastic containers to store silica-dried flowers and foliage.

box is deep, place sturdy dried materials (such as branches and woody seed pods) at the bottom and place fragile flowers at the top. As a precaution, sprinkle in a handful of mothballs and tape the box closed.

For boxes containing glycerin-preserved flowers, punch several holes in each box for improved air circulation. Label the contents of all boxes and store them in a warm, dry location.

Preventing pests

The two most common pests that destroy dried flowers are moths and mice. Moth larvae burrow deep into flower heads, such as strawflowers and peonies. Their voracious chewing can cause entire blooms to fall apart. You can kill the larvae by placing infected dried flowers in a plastic bag and then into a freezer for a couple of days. As a preventative measure, add a few mothballs to your storage containers.

Mice may be a problem if you store your dried flowers in a garage or storage building. They will quickly chew through a cardboard box to get at tasty seed pods and ornamental corn. To prevent damage, set traps and store all your dried materials in ridged plastic containers.

Chapter 3

Design, Tools & Techniques

A flower arrangement begins with an idea, a container, and a few tools. When artfully combined with the spectacular dried blooms of spring and summer, the result is an elegant, long-lasting floral creation.

Hops

Color

Chinese
Lanterns

Sunflowers

FISKARS

Each year our drying shed fills to capacity. Hanging from the lines and stacked in boxes are the dazzling floral ingredients of future arrangements. The sight of all the colors, forms, shapes, and textures might be overwhelming if it weren't for the floral-design principles that help guide us through the arrangement process.

As with any art form, once you understand the basic principles of design, you can begin to experiment and develop your own unique style. This chapter will help you along that path. With a bit of planning, the right tools, and a few tricks of the trade, you can create captivating dried-flower arrangements that will enhance almost any room in your home.

PRINCIPLES OF DESIGN

Understanding the basic principles of floral design is the first step in creating harmonious arrangements. Because the principles are all interrelated, it's important to read the entire design section to have a full overview of the concepts and how they work together. As you gain an eye for color, proportion, rhythm, and balance, you can experiment and develop your own personal style. Keep in mind that flower arranging is subjective; there is no right or wrong way to approach this art form. Use the following concepts and methods as a starting point—experiment, have fun, and design creatively.

Placement

Before you begin an arrangement, decide where it will be placed in your home. The color, scale, and style of the setting will influence your floral design.

Coordinating arrangements with their surroundings is particularly important with dried flowers (unlike fresh flowers that wilt in a week or two).

Flower arrangements should reflect and complement a room's color scheme and furniture style (casual, formal, etc.). If you are creating holiday decorations, choose an arrangement style that blends with your décor but let the colors, textures, and accessories echo the season.

The scale of a room and its furnishing also influence the design and proportion of arrangements. For example, a large, flamboyant arrangement looks top-heavy perched on a small end table. Conversely, a 10-in. wreath looks lost on a large, expansive wall.

The placement of your arrangement also influences its shape. An arrangement's location in a room dictates whether it will be viewed from all sides or from only one side. In general, asymmetrical designs are usually viewed from one side, whereas symmetrical designs are either viewed from one side or all sides.

Backgrounds are also an important consideration. For instance, placing an arrangement in front of a mirror is the same as viewing it from all sides, so all views of the arrangement need to be equally pleasing. Wallpaper patterns can present another placement challenge. A colorful, highly textured arrangement may be lost against a busy print in the same colors.

Not every area in your home is suitable for displaying dried flowers. Humidity and direct sunlight will wilt and fade dried arrangements, so avoid placing them near windows or in steamy bathrooms.

Even though dried-flower arrangements can last for months (if not years), dust and ambient light will eventually take their toll. Discard arrangements before they look old and faded.

This glass bowl filled with roses and tulips complements the floral bedspread. Its size is proportionate with the small nightstand, and its symmetrical design reflects nicely in the mirror.

Containers

Containers are one of the most important components of arrangements. They help establish the style, mood, and size of your design. Because dried flowers don't require water, you can choose from a wide assortment of baskets, bowls, vases, and pots.

To create unified arrangements, the size, shape, and height of a container must be in proportion with the overall design and setting. A container's style and texture must also be compatible with the arrangement and setting. For example, if you are creating a formal atmosphere, use containers made from reflective materials such as silver, porcelain, or glass (see p. 73 for arranging dried flowers in glass containers). Casual, earthy styles are created with containers made from rough, nonreflective materials like baskets, earthenware, and wood. To give your designs personality, consider unconventional containers such as hollowed-out gourds, large seashells, or even ballet slippers.

Color

Color is one of the first design elements you notice in a flower arrangement. Color can set the mood of an arrangement and enhance several design principles including focal point, depth, rhythm, and harmony, all of which will be discussed in this chapter. But first, it's important to understand the basics of color theory and how to combine colors so you can use this design element to its fullest.

Color wheel Understanding color theory begins with understanding a color wheel. A color wheel, shown in the drawing on p. 52, is composed of 12 equal sections. Red, yellow, and blue are the primary colors and cannot be achieved by mixing any other colors. Mixing two primary colors together

From formal to rustic, a wide assortment of containers is suitable for dried-flower arrangements.

in equal amounts produces the secondary colors: green, orange, and violet. The six remaining sections on the wheel are the tertiary, or intermediate, colors: yellow-orange, yellow-green, blue-green, blue-violet, red-violet, and red-orange. They are obtained by mixing adjacent primary and secondary colors. By altering the proportions of each hue being mixed, a near-infinite spectrum of colors is possible.

A color in its purest form is called a hue. The value of a color refers to its lightness or darkness. For example, if you add black to a pure hue it becomes a shade. Adding white makes it a tint, while adding gray results in a tone. The six sections on the color wheel between yellow-green and red represent warm colors. The six sections between green and red-violet are cool colors.

Color schemes The inspiration for a floral arrangement color scheme can come from a variety

Yellow-orange Yellow

Orange Yellow-green

Red-orange Green

Red Blue-green

Red-violet Blue

Violet Blue-violet

Left: *This collection of red-violet flowers creates a vibrant monochromatic color scheme.*

Above: *Blue-violet asters and larkspur combine with yellow-orange marigolds, dahlias, ornamental corn, and dried leaves for a complementary fall color scheme.*

of sources, such as traditional holiday colors, room colors, or printed fabrics. Nature is an unending source of inspiration, with its seasonal colors, sunsets, and the patchwork hues of a cottage garden. While color combinations are evident wherever you look, the following color schemes can be used as a starting point for your designs.

Monochromatic color schemes consist of a single hue and encompass all the related tints, shades, and tones (see the left photo above). For example, an arrangement based on an orange color scheme might include the burnt-orange shades of autumn leaves, the bright orange of Chinese lanterns, and the peach tints of 'Sunset' statice. Green leaves and stems are the only elements that keep these floral arrangements from being purely monochromatic.

However, monochromatic color schemes can become monotonous. Enliven them by bending the rules slightly and adding a hint of white or a small amount of a complementary color. For instance, add white baby's breath for a bit of brightness in an all-blue arrangement, or brighten a spring design of lavender lilacs, larkspur, and statice with a few small, yellow daffodils.

Combining colors directly opposite each other on the color wheel creates **complementary** color schemes. For example, yellow and violet are complementary colors, as are blue and orange. The appearance of these contrasts can be either vivid or subtle depending on the color values (see the right photo above). Pale yellow lilies, for instance, combine with light violet lilacs for a subtle, soft appearance. But the mix of deep-blue delphinium and bright-orange marigolds creates a vibrant contrast. Mixing light and dark values is another way to combine complementary colors—consider deep-purple statice arranged with light-yellow pansies.

Create **analogous** color schemes by combining colors that are directly next to each other on the color wheel, for example, red-violet, violet and blue-violet, or yellow, yellow-orange, and orange. Analogous color schemes evoke a feeling of harmony because the colors are so closely related (see the left photo on p. 54). It's important to use a range of values, from deep shades to light tints, to keep these color schemes lively.

Polychromatic color schemes use any or all of the colors in the spectrum (see the right photo on p. 54).

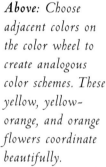

Above: Choose adjacent colors on the color wheel to create analogous color schemes. These yellow, yellow-orange, and orange flowers coordinate beautifully.

Right: This bright assortment of multi-colored flowers illustrates a poly-chromatic color scheme.

While bright multicolored arrangements look festive, they can also appear busy and chaotic. For a softer appearance, design a multicolored composition using a variety of flowers in pale pastels.

Texture

Texture is another important element to consider before you begin arranging. From soft and fuzzy to spiny and rough, plants come in a range of textures that is almost as vast as the color spectrum.

The surface texture of the container you choose, the flowers and foliage, and any accompanying accessories must all interact harmoniously (see the photo on the facing page). For example, create a casual arrangement by combining the rough texture of a willow basket with the coarse, earthy characteristics of seed pods, ornamental grasses, and sunflowers. The use of willow branches as line material will echo the rough texture of the willow basket. Using a variety of textures and repeating them throughout your arrangement will increase interest. The use of texture is especially important in monochromatic arrangements where the element of color contrasts is removed.

Basic arrangement shapes

Visualize an overall shape before you begin arranging. Triangles, circles, ovals, squares, vertical and horizontal rectangles, crescents, and fan shapes are some of the basic geometric shapes that define freestanding flower arrangements.

The overall shape of an arrangement must complement and blend with its surroundings. For example, a horizontal rectangle is perfect for a dinner-table centerpiece. The long, rectangular silhouette repeats the shape of the table, and its low profile does not obscure the dinner guests' views. On the other hand, a large, fan-shaped arrangement works well in front of the opening of an unlit fireplace. See the sidebar on p. 56 for examples of arrangement shapes.

Focal point

A captivating arrangement begins with the selection of focal-point materials. Depending on the mood you want to evoke, the focal area can be either subtle or dramatic, but in either case should draw the viewer's attention. For example, a soft gathering of pale-pink cabbage roses can be just as captivating as a bold focal point composed of large, yellow sunflowers.

The focal area is accentuated through the use of varying shapes, textures, sizes, and colors. Large focal-point flowers draw more attention than smaller accent materials, just as brightly colored focal-point flowers stand out against a background of muted accent flowers. For further emphasis, use warm and cool colors in combination to create the illusion of depth. For instance, bright-yellow focal-point flowers are visually stimulating and will move to the foreground if blue accent flowers, which are visually calming and tend to recede, surround them.

Because focal-point materials are usually the largest and heaviest components in an arrangement, they look balanced when they are the visual center of gravity. For this reason, the focal area is normally placed near the container rim. Traditionally, focal point materials are centrally placed in symmetrical designs and located just off-center in asymmetrical compositions.

Rhythm

Once the viewer is initially attracted to the focal point of your arrangement, it's the use of progressively smaller and lighter materials (line materials, accent materials, and foliage) that carries his attention rhythmically upward and outward through the composition.

Repeating elements produce pleasing rhythms in your design. Use radiating lines to create visual pathways that move the eye from the focal area to the edges of the composition and back again. In addition, repeating colors, textures, and flower types will add to the rhythm, as will gradual transitions in the color and size of the plant materials.

Balance

Well-balanced arrangements, both physically and visually, are easy to enjoy because they satisfy our need for equilibrium. To prevent an arrangement from toppling, the physical weight of the plant materials must be evenly distributed over the container. Keep the majority of the weight centered and near the rim.

Even though dried materials are light and probably won't topple an arrangement, their visual weight must look balanced. This is easy to achieve in a symmetrical composition. In asymmetrical designs, there must be an even distribution of plant materials on either side of the central axis.

Proportion

Proportion is closely related to balance and refers to the relationship between the plant materials and the container, as well as the relationship between the

Rough textures usually convey a casual appearance, while soft textures can help to evoke a subtle, formal ambiance.

ARRANGEMENT SHAPES

Every arrangement has a silhouette, and most traditional arrangements are based on geometric shapes or combinations of geometric shapes. Most freestanding arrangements fall into three silhouette categories: mass, line, and line-mass.

MASS ARRANGEMENTS

The mass arrangement style is commonly used for dried flowers because it helps conceal wired stems. The silhouettes resemble loose geometric forms, including triangles, circles, rectangles, ovals, and fan shapes. Mass designs are usually symmetrical. Although they can be one-sided, they are often viewed from all sides and lack a central focal point.

LINE ARRANGEMENTS

Most line arrangements have tall vertical silhouettes. They are usually one-sided and asymmetrical in design. The use of tall, narrow containers allows you to radiate line materials out from the focal area (both above and below the rim of the container) to accentuate the linear silhouette.

LINE-MASS ARRANGEMENTS

Line-mass arrangements are a combination of line and mass silhouettes. In general the mass portion of the composition is centered near the rim of the container, while the line materials radiate outward. Line-mass arrangements can be either symmetrical or asymmetrical.

individual components within the arrangement. To establish a correctly proportioned design, decide how far your plant materials should extend above and to the sides of your container. Use your eye to determine the correct proportion. When it's correct, the arrangement will be pleasing to view; if the design is incorrectly proportioned, it will look unbalanced. While your eye is the best judge, here's a general rule of thumb to use as a starting point for arrangements that are taller than they are wide. The height of an arrangement above the container should be 1½ to 2 times the height of the container.

Consider the scale of the individual components within an arrangement as well. While varying plant sizes create interest in floral designs, extreme size differences look out of proportion.

TOOLS AND SUPPLIES

Dried-flower arranging is a rewarding pastime if you have a comfortable work area and the correct tools and supplies. Choose an area with good lighting and plenty of room to spread out your materials. Most flower arranging is done from a standing position, so use a table that is a comfortable work height. Protect the surface with a mat or a sheet of plywood or cardboard (accidental glue-gun drips and scratches from clippers and wires are a common occurrence). The following is a list of helpful flower-arranging tools and supplies (available at most craft stores).

Floral tape: Floral tape is used to wrap wires or bind wires to stems. It comes in a range of colors including white, brown, and shades of green. Although it's not an adhesive tape, its wax coating clings to itself when the tape is stretched.

Floral adhesive tape: Floral adhesive tape (sometimes called waterproof or anchor tape) is used to secure foam blocks to containers.

Glue guns: Hot-glue guns come in a variety of sizes and temperature ranges. They are all suitable for dried-flower arranging.

Floral clay: Floral clay has a putty-like consistency and is generally used to affix floral foam to containers.

Wire: Floral wire comes in different lengths and gauges. For most projects, we use 12-in., 21-gauge wire. It also comes rolled on spools or paddles (handy for making wreaths and garlands). We prefer floral wire coated with green enamel paint because it blends with the plant materials and resists rust.

Picks: Wooden floral picks are pointed at one end and have a thin wire attached to the other. They are used to anchor accessories or small bundles of flowers to arrangements, garlands, and wreaths.

Greening pins: Greening pins are used to secure moss to floral foam or wreath forms. You can purchase pins or make your own by cutting 21-gauge wire into 4-in. lengths and bending them into a hairpin shape.

Clippers, shears, and scissors: Use a good pair of hand shears or clippers to cut dry flower stems. If you are cutting branches or woody stems, use pruning shears or loppers. Trim ribbon with a sharp pair of household or sewing scissors.

Knives: A long-bladed kitchen knife is used to cut and shape floral foam, while a pocketknife is handy for cutting stems.

Your eye is by far the best judge of proportion, but a general rule of thumb is to make the arrangement 1½ times the height of its container.

Have your tools and supplies close at hand before you begin an arrangement. It's also a good idea to protect your work surface from accidental glue-gun drips with a mat or piece of cardboard.

Candles, ribbon, and imitation fruit are just a few accessories that add personality to your arrangements.

Wire cutters: Medium-size diagonal wire cutters will easily cut through floral wire without straining your hand.

Floral foam: Floral foam is the sturdy base material into which flower stems are inserted. Floral foam specifically made for fresh flowers is green and absorbs water. Foam blocks made for dried-flower arranging are usually brown (sometimes green) and similar to finely textured Styrofoam.

Moss: Moss is used to conceal floral foam and wreath forms and is available in two colors. Depending on the color scheme of your arrangement, use either green sphagnum moss or gray Spanish moss.

Surface sealers: Spray sealers help prevent dried plant materials from shattering and reabsorbing moisture.

Colored floral sprays: Specially formulated floral spray paints are used to enhance the colors of plant materials.

Accessories: Accessories are the extra touches that add personality to arrangements. They may include old garden tools, flower pots, bird eggs, imitation fruit, or seashells, to name a few. Use large accessories, such as imitation fruit, as focal points, or intersperse smaller accessories, such as seashells, to carry a theme. Two of the most common accessories are ribbon and candles. Use ribbon only as an accent—let the flowers be the focus of your design. Ribbons should blend with the color scheme, style, and proportion of your arrangements. Candlelight will enhance your holiday decorations and dinner-table centerpieces, but be in attendance when a dried-flower arrangement contains lighted candles.

TECHNIQUES

Learning a few tricks will help you create attractive, long-lasting dried-flower arrangements. The following techniques will save you time and ensure your arrangements are well constructed with the freshest-looking dried flowers possible.

Using surface sealers

Surface sealers prevent delicate dried flowers from shattering and rehydrating. Traditional everlastings, such as statice, strawflowers, and globe amaranth, have stiff, papery petals and do not require surface sealers. But it is necessary to seal delicate flowers such as lilacs, tulips, and anemones. As a general rule, seal all silica-dried flowers and foliage.

Spray sealers made specifically for dried flowers are available at craft stores. Although spray sealers' light consistency provides an excellent base coat and often prevents petals from curling, most silica-dried flowers require additional sealing coats for rigidity. Over the base coat we apply fast-drying clear satin spray polyurethane (available at hardware stores). If you have difficulty finding floral sealers, spray polyurethane may be adequate for all applications; however, we have found the combination works best.

To help prevent the flower petals from curling, apply several *light* coats rather than a single, liberal application. Despite using this technique, some delicate flower petals may still curl. Sometimes this can be prevented by carefully gluing petals together before they are sprayed (see p. 61 for details).

Most sealers are toxic and should be used outdoors or in a well-ventilated area (read all product labels for additional warnings). We prefer to work outdoors on warm days with low humidity.

To seal flowers you will need:

- a work table
- rubber gloves
- one or two blocks of floral foam
- waxed paper
- a small artist's paintbrush
- spray sealer(s)
- an assortment of dried materials

1. If you are sealing with silica gel, use a small paintbrush to carefully dust any residual silica gel off the dried flowers. If you are sealing air-dried materials, skip to step 2.
2. Wearing rubber gloves, hold a single blossom at arm's length and lightly spray the backside of the bloom with a base coat of floral sealer.
3. If the flower is attached to a stem or wire, insert it into a block of foam to dry. If you are sealing just a flower head, place the bloom facedown on

Use surface sealers and colored floral sprays outside or in well-ventilated areas.

a sheet of waxed paper to dry. Repeat these steps for the remaining blooms.

4. When the flowers are dry, spray the face of each one. Make sure the sealer reaches well into the center of each bloom. Allow the flowers to dry before moving on to the next step.
5. Repeat the process using spray polyurethane. Allow the sealer to dry between applications. Build up several light coats on the back and face of each flower until the petals feel stiff and leathery. After the final coat of sealer has dried, apply colored floral sprays.

Using colored floral sprays

Dried flowers never remain as colorful as they were the day they were harvested. Drying and exposure to light often changes and fades their natural colors. Fortunately, the floral industry has developed paints specifically for flowers. Unlike ordinary spray paint, colored floral sprays have a light consistency that imparts a natural look to dried flowers and foliage (see the photo below).

Some flowers, including statice, strawflowers, and larkspur, hold their natural colors well and do not require spraying. Others, such as bells of Ireland, lilacs, amaranth, and most leaves, fade quickly and benefit from colored sprays.

While most blooms need two or three different colors to appear natural, some plant materials (especially foliage) can be sprayed with a single color and look fairly realistic. Here we'll explain the basic principles of applying colored floral sprays; experimentation and observation of fresh flowers, though, produces the best results.

Use the same basic supplies and work space as mentioned on p. 59 for applying surface sealers. Have an assortment of colored floral sprays that match the natural colors of the materials to be sprayed. The following example explains the techniques for creating a fresh-looking lilac. Use these same spray techniques (with different colors) to enhance all your dried-plant materials.

1. Wearing rubber gloves, hold a lilac by its stem at arm's length. Lightly spray a dark-violet base coat color over the entire bloom. Rotate the flower to ensure even coverage and to avoid runs and drips.
2. Apply a slightly lighter shade of violet. Pulse the spray nozzle in short bursts while rotating the blossom to produce a lightly mottled effect. This gives the flower interest and depth.
3. Finally, apply a light-lavender color. Hold the spray can about 12 in. away from the flower and tilt the lilac almost perpendicular to the can. Pulse

Colored floral sprays make an obvious impact. Here are lilacs (left), bells of Ireland (center), and amaranth (right) before and after applying colored floral sprays.

the spray nozzle in short bursts while rotating the flower to tint just the edges of the individual florets, creating the effect of highlights.

Wiring

Floral wire is indispensable for dried-flower arranging. It is commonly used for binding and attaching materials onto wreaths and garlands and for fashioning artificial stems.

We use 12-in., 21-gauge wire to create "stems" for the flower heads of sea holly and strawflower. To wire a flower head, cut the stem close to the bloom (leave about ⅛ in. of stem attached). Insert a wire about ¼ in. into the end of the freshly cut stem (see the photo at right). If you insert the wire too far, it will protrude from the blossom's center. Dry the wired flowers standing upright in a coffee can or similar container. As the stem dries around the wire, it forms a tight bond.

Taping

Floral tape is used to camouflage wire stems and to bind flowers and foliage onto wires. With practice, wrapping wires with floral tape takes very little time. Begin by grasping the end of the tape and the top of a wire between your thumb and forefinger. Roll the tape and wire between your fingers in one direction while gently stretching the tape downward with your other hand, as shown in the top photo on p. 62. As the tape winds in a spiral, it covers the wire.

Use the combination of tape and wire to extend and strengthen stems. If a dried-flower stem is too weak to hold up its flower head or too short, place a wire along the length of the stem and tape the two together. Even though dried-flower stems can be artificially extended, it is important to re-create a flower's

natural stem length for a realistic appearance.

You can also tape small bundles of flowers or foliage onto wires. We often group three leaves of dusty miller or lamb's ears together and tape them to a wire for easy insertion into garlands, wreaths, arrangements.

Using picks

Floral picks anchor accessories to wreaths, garlands, and arrangements. They also extend and strengthen stems. To secure accessories to an arrangement (such as ornamental corn or pinecones) simply wrap the pick's wire around the base of the accessory until the pick is firmly attached.

Similarly, use the wire to bind flowers with short, weak stems onto a pick for added strength. This method is also ideal for binding small bundles of flowers to picks for insertion into wreaths and garlands (see the bottom photo on p. 62).

Although accessories such as small pumpkins and gourds are perishable, they can be temporarily secured to a dried arrangement with picks. Begin by removing the thin wire. Plunge the pointed end of the pick into a small pumpkin or gourd and insert the protruding end of the pick into a foam or wreath base.

Gluing and reconstructing stems

A hot-glue gun is indispensable for dried-flower arranging. Its numerous uses include attaching flowers to wires and stems, gluing accessories onto wreaths, repairing shattered blooms, and securing floral foam to containers.

Insert wires into freshly harvested strawflower and eryngium blossoms for sturdy, artificial stems.

The point of a hot-glue gun is small enough to dispense the right amount of glue for most projects. However, it may be too large for replacing broken petals or gluing petals together for support. For these delicate jobs, place a drop of hot glue on the tip of a toothpick and apply it where needed.

Hot-glue guns are ideal for reconstructing flower stems and attaching flower heads to wires. To create a wire stem for a silica-dried flower head, glue the flower's short length of natural stem along one end of a 12-in., 21-gauge wire. When the glue is dry, wrap the wire stem with floral tape.

Extra time and patience are required to reconstruct an entire stem (stem, leaves, and flowers), but the realistic results will reward your effort. The following technique works well with peonies.

To reconstruct a complete peony stem, you will need:
- silica gel
- 21-gauge wire
- colored floral sprays and surface sealers
- a hot-glue gun
- a block of floral foam
- a peony plant

Floral tape comes in a range of colors that will help conceal wire stems in arrangements.

Use floral picks to attach accessories and small bundles of flowers to arrangements, wreaths, and garlands.

1. Harvest the flower head in late spring when it is in full bloom. Dry the blossom in silica gel.
2. Once the foliage has matured in late summer, cut the main stem near the soil line. Remove the foliage by cutting the leaf stems close to the main stem. Dry the foliage in silica gel.
3. While the stem is fresh, insert 1-in. lengths of 21-gauge wire into the main stem where each leaf was removed. In addition, insert one 1-in. length of wire at the top of the stem where the

bloom was removed. The wires should protrude from the stem approximately ¾ in. (see the photo at right). Air-dry the stem.

4. When the leaves, stem, and blossom are dry, apply surface sealers and colored floral sprays.

5. Start the reconstruction by inserting the stem into a block of floral foam for stability. Begin at the base of the stem and place a small bead of hot glue on the lowest protruding wire. Immediately push a leaf stem onto the wire. While the glue is still hot, quickly adjust the leaf position for a natural appearance. Work your way up the stem repeating the process for each leaf. Finally, use the same technique to attach the flower head to the top wire.

Similar techniques can be used with hollyhocks, dogwood branches, lilies, asters, and roses. Insert wires into the stem ends for reattaching the flower heads, or simply glue the flower head onto the stems ends. The same is true for the leaves. Either insert wires into the leaf joints and glue the leaves onto the wires, or simply glue the leaves onto the stem.

This technique also works well for gluing flower heads onto surrogate stems. If a particular plant stem does not dry well, dry the flower head and glue it to the dried stem of another plant. In arrangements where stems will show, use surrogate stems in place of wire stems.

Cutting floral foam and applying moss

Floral foam is the base material for most dried arrangements. Use a long-bladed kitchen knife to cut the material. Assess your container opening and cut the foam block to fit snugly. To position stems horizontally or slightly downward, the foam should

Use a hot-glue gun to secure flower heads onto wires and to reconstruct stems.

extend ½ in. to 1 in. above the rim. Bevel the edges that protrude above the container.

If the foam is smaller than the container opening, use hot glue to permanently attach the block to the bottom of the container. However, if you eventually want to remove your arrangement from its container, secure the foam with floral adhesive tape, floral clay, or wires (to prevent wires from cutting into the floral foam, position wooden picks along the edges.

Finally, conceal the foam beneath a light layer of moss. Secure the moss to the foam with several greening pins. If the moss is dry and crumbly, lightly spray it with warm water for easy handling.

PART TWO

CELEBRATING
THE SEASONS

Chapter 4

Spring Arrangements

Spring-flowering bulbs are rarely thought of as dried flowers, but their ephemeral beauty can easily be preserved. With a bit of patience you can turn these and other spring flowers into elegant, enduring arrangements.

SPRING BULB POTS

MATERIALS LIST

40 cattail leaves

30 scarlet-seeded iris leaves

Floral foam

*1 terra-cotta flowerpot and
saucer (5 in. dia.)*

*1 square terra-cotta planter
(9½ in. x 4½ in. x 4½ in.)*

Moss

3 blue hyacinths

*16 assorted daffodil blossoms
and buds*

Pea gravel

Short length of sisal twine

Most of the bulbs you plant in the fall will faithfully bloom the following spring, but the tenure of their floral display is always fleeting. Why not enjoy spring flowers year-round with these delightfully deceiving bulb pots?

We began this project by gathering a beautiful collection of silica-dried daffodils and a trio of hyacinths. While preserving the flowers of these spring bulbs was fairly easy, drying their foliage presented a greater challenge. Daffodil and hyacinth leaves do not dry well, so we came up with believable substitutes. Cattail and iris leaves are wonderful foliage look-alikes for these plants and remain sturdy after drying. Cattail leaves shrink in width as they air-dry, reducing them to the size of daffodil foliage, while scarlet-seeded iris leaves make perfect mock hyacinth foliage with a bit of trimming.

1. ♦ To create the daffodil leaves, air-dry cattail foliage at room temperature, then round off the tips with scissors, as shown at left in the photo. Create the hyacinth foliage by rounding off the tips of scarlet-seeded iris leaves while they are fresh. Partially fill a microwave-safe dish with silica gel, and push the edges of all the leaves into the crystals, curving and bending the leaves as shown. Cover them with additional silica gel, and dry them in the microwave (see pp. 42-43 for details). Spray the cattail and iris foliage with a surface sealer and green floral spray.

2. ♦ Cut blocks of floral foam to fit the terra-cotta containers. Cut the foam for the square hyacinth planter so it sits ¾ in. below the rim, leaving room for the pea gravel in step 5. Cut the foam for the round daffodil pot even with the rim, and cover it with moss.

3. ♦ Spray the hyacinths with surface sealers and 1 or 2 shades of blue floral spray. Insert the blossoms into the floral foam in a straight row, then insert the foliage into the foam so it radiates from the base of each stem (approximately 10 leaves per blossom).

4. ♦ Apply green floral spray to the daffodil stems, and spray the blooms with surface sealers and yellow floral spray if necessary. Even with light spray applications, some petals may slightly curl. This curling will be less noticeable once the flowers

are grouped in the arrangement. To make the arrangement, start in the center of the pot, and insert a selection of flowers and foliage into the foam base. Work your way toward the edges of the pot until you have a pleasing cluster of flowers and foliage.

DRYING DAFFODILS AND HYACINTHS

Before drying daffodils and hyacinths in silica gel, strengthen their stems with wire. Do this by simply inserting a 12-in., 21-gauge wire into the cut end of the stem.

For hyacinths: Slowly push the wire up the center of the stem until it reaches the top (it may be necessary to bend the stem as you push to keep the wire centered).

For daffodils: Gently bend the flower head in line with the stem, and slowly push the wire until it reaches the center of the flower head. Once the wire is inserted, bend the base of the flower head back to its original 90-degree angle. For varieties with multiple flower heads, insert one wire for each flower head (up to 3 wires per stem).

The flowers are now ready to dry on their sides in silica gel (see pp. 41-42 for details).

$5.$ Complete the daffodil pot by adding a sisal tie and a terra-cotta saucer. Finish the hyacinth container by concealing the floral foam beneath a layer of pea gravel.

EVERLASTING ILLUSION

MATERIALS LIST

7 pink roses (with reconstructed stems)

1 glass bowl (5 in. dia.)

5 green hellebores

6 white tulips

4 pink roses (flower heads only)

24 oz. clear floral resin (with mixing and pouring supplies, see steps 4 and 5)

Create an extraordinary display of fresh-looking dried flowers by placing them in a glass bowl filled with "water." This lush gathering of silica-dried tulips, hellebores, and roses is perfect for this fresh-cut ruse because of their long stems and vibrant colors. The stems are actually submerged in a crystal-clear floral resin that looks like water but sets up hard in 24 to 48 hours.

While this technique is not hard, it does require patience and a steady hand. As you arrange, keep the glass vase free of debris or the debris will be encased in the resin. It is also important to use materials that are perfectly dry; glycerin-preserved materials are not suitable for this technique.

1. ♦ To reconstruct the stems of 7 pink roses, start by spraying the rose flower heads with surface sealers, then apply surface sealers and green floral spray to the foliage. Reconstruct each stem by gluing on a flower head and 1 or 2 leaves toward the top (see pp. 61-63 for details). Arrange the rose stems in the clean glass bowl so the flower heads extend just beyond the rim. To prevent the stems from tipping out, temporarily clip the foliage together with small alligator clips (use small clips so they don't crush the dry foliage). Make sure the stem ends are near the bottom of the vase.

3. ♦ Spray the white tulips with surface sealers, and insert them randomly throughout the arrangement. Fill in any gaps in the design with the 4 remaining rose flower heads by gluing them to surrounding leaves and stems.

2. ♦ Spray the hellebores with surface sealers and green floral spray. Evenly distribute them throughout the arrangement so they form a mounded shape. The goal is to have all the visible stems in the vase appear as though they are receiving "water," so the stems should either reach the bottom of the vase or be cut short so they are not visible within the glass container.

4. Once the arrangement is complete, set it aside and assemble the materials necessary for mixing the clear floral resin. You will need a disposable stir stick, a glass container, and a pair of rubber or latex gloves. Protect your work surface with a sheet of plywood or heavy cardboard. Read the pamphlet that comes with the resin.

5. Set the arrangement on a protected work surface in an area where it can be left undisturbed. Wearing rubber gloves, mix the resin as stated in the instruction pamphlet. Using a long funnel, carefully pour the resin

into the vase (inexpensive, long funnels can be found at automotive stores). Be careful not to disturb the flowers or break off any debris into the resin.

6. Allow the arrangement to stand undisturbed for 24 to 48 hours or until the resin sets up. When the resin is hard, remove the alligator clips.

EASTER GARLAND

MATERIALS LIST

10 eggs

Assorted acrylic craft paints

36 salal sprigs (fresh)

Green sisal twine (6 ft.)

2 or 3 hop vines

Cream ribbon (4 yd. x 1½ in.)

34 daffodils in a variety of sizes

20 small baby's breath sprigs

This year, decorate your home for Easter with this easy-to-make garland. Endowed with bright yellow daffodils, it will light up any room. It also gives you the opportunity to display a collection of hand-decorated Easter eggs. The completed garland can hang from a mantle, above a window, or even on a wall above a buffet table for Easter Sunday brunch.

We used salal sprigs for the base of our garland, but almost any greenery that dries well—boxwood, hop vines, or the pods of money plant—will work. Your local florist may be a good source for fresh greens that you can dry at home. Make the fresh garland base at least 2 weeks ahead of the holiday so it has plenty of time to dry at room temperature.

1. Using a pin or a thin metal skewer, carefully poke holes in both ends of each egg. Over a sink, blow out the egg whites and yokes, then rinse and dry the eggshells. When the eggs are completely dry, apply a base coat of acrylic craft paint (we used various shades of green). To avoid touching the freshly painted eggs, insert a wire into one of the holes in each egg, and insert the other end into a block of floral foam. Once the base coat is dry, decorate the eggs with acrylic paints. We decorated our eggs with simple patterns in contrasting white paint.

2. To create the leafy garland base, use 22-gauge wire to bind the salal sprigs onto green sisal twine. Overlap each foliage sprig as you progress along the twine. Once your garland reaches 6 ft. long, cut the twine and wire. Make 2 wire loops, and attach them to the garland at your chosen hanging points. Hang the garland on a wall, and allow it to dry at room temperature for 1 to 2 weeks. Once the garland is dry, remove it from the wall and apply green floral sprays.

3. Hang the garland in its final position. Cut the hop vines into 18 small sprigs, then glue on the sprigs to fill in any gaps and to give the garland a full appearance. Make and attach 2 ribbon bows with long tails at the hanging points (see p. 157 for directions on making bows).

4. Next, glue on your decorated eggs. Evenly distribute them throughout the garland, and glue them directly onto the foliage.

5. Before you position the daffodils, apply surface sealers to the front and back of each bloom. Keep the applications light, but apply several coats. Some petals may curl in the process but the curls will be less noticeable once all the flowers are in place. Position the largest daffodils first, followed by the medium size, and finally the smallest. Make sure some daffodils are positioned at the base of the eggs to give the eggs visual support.

6. To complete your Easter garland, tuck in delicate sprigs of baby's breath. Keep the clusters small for a light and airy appearance.

ROSE BUD VASE

MATERIALS LIST

1 bud vase (8 in. tall)

Floral foam

Moss

*Assorted sprigs of delicate foliage
or fern fronds*

*5 pink roses with reconstructed
stems (at various stages of
development)*

6 pink astilbe

*3 wax-leaf privet flower
clusters in bud*

It's possible to create a beautiful bud vase arrangement with just a few blossoms from your garden. This delicate vase of roses provides a perfect accent for a nightstand, vanity table, or memento shelf. The great advantage of dried flowers is the ability to convey the essence of a season with flowers that bloom at different times of the year. For example, the roses we chose for this bud vase actually bloom in early summer, but their light pink color combined with cream-colored wax-leaf privet flower buds and delicate fern fronds reminds us of spring.

Any delicate leaves or fern fronds that dry well are appropriate for this small arrangement. We used two types of foliage that grow wild in our woods: the leaves of the inside-out flower (*Vancouveria hexandra*) and the fronds of the Western maidenhair fern (*Adiantum pedatum*).

1. ♦ Cut a small wedge of floral foam from a larger block. Shape the foam so it fits snugly in the bud vase and rises slightly above the rim, then cover the foam with moss.

3. ♦ Spray the rose flower heads with surface sealers, then apply surface sealers and green floral spray to the foliage. Reconstruct each stem by gluing on a flower head and 1 or 2 leaves toward the top (see pp. 61-63 for details). Insert each stem into the foam base, starting with the fully open bloom near the rim followed by increasingly tighter blossoms toward the top of the arrangement.

2. ♦ Spray the foliage with surface sealers and green floral spray. If necessary, lengthen their stems with tape and wire. Insert several foliage sprigs into the foam base, keeping the arrangement of the foliage loose so the resulting design has a light and airy appearance. (If necessary, extra foliage can be added later to fill in any obvious gaps.)

4. ◆ Spray the astilbe flower spikes with surface sealers. If necessary, lengthen their stems with tape and wire. Position the flower spikes so they extend slightly above the roses.

5. ◆ Glue and tape wire stems onto the wax-leaf privet flower clusters, and spray them with surface sealers. These flower-bud clusters are beautiful; however, they are very fragile and must be arranged carefully. Insert the wire stems into the foam base so the flowers are positioned in the center of the design.

6. ◆ Finish the bud vase arrangement by adding small sprigs of foliage to fill in any gaps in the design.

SPRING CELEBRATION

*1 blue-and-white vase
(9 in. dia.)*

Floral foam

Moss

11 salal sprigs

10 green hellebore sprigs

6 blue hyacinths

13 white tulips

This blue-and-white composition combines three of spring's premier blossoms: tulips, hyacinths, and hellebores. Perfect for a desk or a dining table, its symmetrical design allows it to be viewed from all sides. The simple composition and color combination of this arrangement make it easy to re-create yet evoke a feeling of elegance.

You can enjoy the fresh flowers for this arrangement long before you harvest them for drying. The evergreen foliage and early blossoms of hellebores will provide interest in your winter landscape, while tulips will brighten your early spring flowerbeds. Grow hyacinths indoors (in pots or in hyacinth glasses) to enjoy their heady fragrance until they are at their peak of perfection and ready to harvest.

1. Cut the floral foam to fit your container, then cover the surface with moss, and secure it with greening pins.

2. Apply a light coat of green floral spray to the salal sprigs, then insert the salal into the foam base. Evenly space the stems to form a mound shape, allowing some leaves to drape over the container's edge. Although large areas of the moss will show, the flowers will eventually cover the entire surface.

3. Spray the hellebore sprigs with surface sealers and a light coat of green floral spray. Insert each stem into the foam base so the flowers match the mounded shape established by the salal leaves. Turn the container as you work to ensure the symmetrical placement of the material. To soften the hard edge of the container, allow some of the flowers to spill over the rim.

4. Wire and dry the 6 hyacinths, which are the large focal-point flowers of this arrangement (see the sidebar on p. 71). Spray the dried blossoms with surface sealers and 1 or 2 shades of blue floral spray. Evenly place the hyacinths.

5. Finally, dry the tulips, which are delicate flowers to dry but well worth the effort (see the sidebar above). Once the tulips are dry and surface-sealed, insert the stems into the foam base, evenly distributing the flowers throughout the arrangement.

SPRING INTO SUMMER

MATERIALS LIST

1 wire wreath form (14 in.)

42 salal sprigs (fresh)

*Olive green wire-edged ribbon
(2 yd. x 1½ in.)*

2 or 3 large blue hydrangeas

1 pink peony

1 pink aster

5 purple zinnias

2 purple lilacs

1 white lily

1 white tulip

4 white pompon dahlias

5 bishop's weed

8 green hellebore sprigs

10 purple gomphrena

11 small narcissus

This "garden-fresh" wreath celebrates the transition from spring into summer. With the magic of dried flowers, we brought together a selection of blossoms that represent both seasons, including hellebores, tulips, narcissus, lilacs, peonies, asters, zinnias, and hydrangeas.

The beauty of this wreath comes from its lush appearance and vibrant, harmonious colors. It's not necessary to use the exact ingredients that we did to achieve similar results. If your garden contains a different palette of plants, choose blooms with rich colors that harmonize with each other, and select flowers of varying sizes and textures. Dry them in silica gel to retain their fresh look. Plan ahead if you decide to give this wreath as a gift; the fresh salal wreath base will take at least 2 weeks to air-dry at room temperature.

1. ◆ Use 22-gauge wire to bind fresh salal sprigs onto your wreath form, using the same technique shown on p. 152. Allow the fresh wreath to dry at room temperature for 1 to 2 weeks. When the salal is dry, apply green floral spray to the leaves. Make and attach a bow with long loops and tails (see p. 157 for directions on making bows). Secure a small loop of wire to the wreath form, and hang the wreath on a wall at a comfortable work height.

3. ◆ Next, apply surface sealers and colored floral sprays to the pink and purple flowers: peony, aster, zinnias, and lilacs. Glue and tape each flower head onto a wire, then glue each wire stem onto the wreath form. The wires can be easily bent to face the flower heads in slightly different directions—face some upward, others outward, and create depth by tucking some behind leaves.

2. ◆ Apply 2 or 3 shades of purple and blue floral spray to the hydrangea blossoms. Cut the large hydrangeas into 5 smaller clusters and glue them to the wreath, grouping 2 at the top and 3 at the bottom.

4. Apply surface sealers to all the white flowers: lily, tulip, pompon dahlias, and bishop's weed. Glue and tape the flower heads onto wires. Randomly position the blossoms so the surface of the wreath is covered by an even distribution of flowers, then glue them in place.

5. Spray the hellebore sprigs with surface sealers and green floral spray. Tuck the sprigs among the blossoms, and use them to fill any gaps. They should be positioned so they extend slightly above the other flowers.

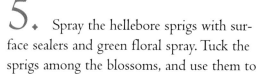

6. Finish the wreath by gluing on gomphrena and small narcissus blooms (we used the cultivar 'Avalanche'). These small flowers look wonderful peeking out from beneath leaves or larger blossoms.

Chapter 5

Summer Arrangements

By midsummer, a kaleidoscopic array of flowers will fill your garden. Dried arrangements created from these vibrant blooms will bring summer indoors and brighten the coldest days of winter.

Hollyhock

SUMMER'S ESSENCE

MATERIALS LIST

1 cast-iron urn (14 in. tall)

Floral foam

Moss

20 salal sprigs

12 purple statice

9 purple lilacs

9 red peonies

9 white dahlias

14 white larkspur

*14 wax-leaf privet flower
clusters in bud*

Y ou can keep the memory of your landscape fresh long into the winter months with this striking memento of summer peonies, lilacs, dahlias, and larkspur. Displayed in a colorful garden setting, this cast-iron urn filled with the beauty of a garden's harvest looks deceivingly fresh, yet all the flowers in this arrangement (and surrounding its base) are crisp to the touch.

An arrangement of this stature is well suited for an entry-hall table or pedestal and can be viewed from all sides. Although the container is formidable, the large, robust blossoms maintain a perfectly proportioned design. In addition, the variety of textures enlivens the simple purple, white, and magenta color scheme.

1. Fill the urn with floral foam, and conceal it with a layer of moss.

2. Apply green floral spray to the salal sprigs, and insert them into the foam base, positioning them so they form a loose conical shape. Insert the stems of purple statice randomly throughout the foliage.

3. Prepare the lilacs by applying surface sealers and 2 or 3 shades of violet and lavender floral spray. Glue the flower heads onto wires or surrogate stems (the salal foliage is dense enough to hide the majority of these stems). Position the lilacs so they radiate from the center of the arrangement and follow the conical shape established by the foliage. They should extend just beyond the tips of the leaves.

4. Apply surface sealers and colored floral sprays to the peonies, and glue them onto wires or their own dried stems. Evenly position them throughout the arrangement.

5. Spray the white dahlias with surface sealers (and floral sprays if necessary), and glue them onto wires or surrogate stems. Nestle them around the peonies and lilacs. Next, insert the white larkspur so they radiate from the center of the design and follow the shape of the arrangement established by the lilacs.

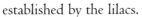

6. Finally, apply surface sealers to the wax-leaf privet flower-bud clusters, then glue and tape them onto wires. Position them randomly throughout the arrangement to give the design a light and airy feel and to fill in any gaps. If wax-leaf privet is not available, use baby's breath, German statice, or sea lavender as a substitute.

NATURE'S SOUVENIRS

MATERIALS LIST

*1 stripped willow wreath
(14 in. dia.)*

4 eucalyptus branches

2 to 4 peegee hydrangea blossoms

14 dusty miller leaves

5 sea holly blossoms

Assorted seashells

Ornamental grass foliage

This soft-hued wreath is reminiscent of summer afternoons spent at the ocean hunting for seashells, sand dollars, and other souvenirs from nature. Even the sparse vegetation of sand dunes is represented in the wispy strands of grass and spiny blossoms of sea holly.

We chose a palette of subtle colors to define this summertime wreath. Air-dried eucalyptus retains its natural sea-foam green color, while the light-gray dusty miller leaves mimic seaweed. The beautiful pale green and coral hydrangea blossoms are a perfect complement to the delicately colored sea urchin shells. To complete the maritime theme, we added airy, gray-green strands of "sea grass," which are actually the leaves of feathertop grass (*Pennisetum villosum*).

1. ♦ Attach a loop of wire to the back of the wreath, and hang it at a comfortable work height. Glue the eucalyptus branches to the wreath following the curve of the form. We used two cultivars of eucalyptus: 'Silver Plate' and 'Silver Dollar'.

2. ♦ Cut the large hydrangea blossoms into small clusters (approximately 20), and glue them to the wreath form.

3. ♦ Glue the dusty miller around the wreath in clusters of 2 or 3 leaves. They look best when their stems are tucked behind the eucalyptus leaves or hydrangea blossoms.

4. ♦ Randomly position and glue the sea holly blossoms in place.

5. Next, position the assorted seashells. If you don't have a collection of seashells, craft stores often carry a nice selection. We chose seashells, sea urchins, and a starfish in a range of subtle colors. Position them randomly among the flowers and foliage, placing the largest shells at the bottom, and glue them in place.

6. Finally, add wispy grass as the finishing touch to this wreath. Use floral tape to bind 3 or 4 strands together at the cut ends, and glue them to the wreath form. Gently bend the individual strands to follow the curve of the form. As you bend the strands, hook them around surrounding flowers, leaves, and seashells to hold them in place. If necessary, lightly tack them with glue.

COTTAGE-GARDEN BASKET

MATERIALS LIST

1 willow basket (7 in. x 8 in. dia.)

Floral foam

Moss

13 peony foliage sprigs

8 lavender ageratum

3 reconstructed hollyhock stems (with multiple pink flowers and buds)

6 cream snapdragons

6 wax-leaf privet flower clusters in bud

8 lilac larkspur

I n the late 19th century, a gardening tradition took root in the English countryside. Rambling roses were used to frame the entryways of thatched-roof cottages, and flowers were planted in natural abundance. It was the beginning of the cottage garden—a romantic garden style that persists to this day.

To capture the essence of this traditional garden style in a dried arrangement, we gathered together the blooms of some old-time garden favorites, including hollyhocks, snapdragons, and larkspur. A charming willow basket is reminiscent of simple country craftsmanship and proved to be the ideal container for this cottage-garden bouquet.

We designed this arrangement to be viewed from one side; however, it could be viewed from all sides by inserting a few additional stems of ageratum, snapdragons, larkspur, and wax-leaf privet.

1. ♦ Fill the basket to its rim with floral foam, and conceal it with a layer of moss. Apply a surface sealer and green floral spray to the peony foliage, then insert the sprigs into the foam base.

3. ♦ Before you reconstruct the hollyhock stems, which are the focal points of this arrangement, spray the individual flowers, buds, and stems with surface sealers and colored floral sprays. Glue the flowers and buds onto the stems. Insert the tallest stem into the center of the arrangement, followed by the 2 shorter stems on either side.

2. ♦ Spray the ageratum blossoms with surface sealers and lavender floral spray. Insert them into the foam base among the peony foliage.

4. Next, spray the snapdragons with surface sealers. Colored floral sprays are optional because snap-dragons usually hold their colors well after drying. Position them so they follow the conical shape of the arrangement.

5. Spray the wax-leaf privet flower buds with surface sealers, and position them randomly throughout the arrangement.

6. Finally, insert the lilac larkspur throughout the arrangement. Position them so they follow the shape of the design and extend slightly above the surrounding flowers.

SUMMER SAMPLER

MATERIALS LIST

*1 wicker hamper (14 in. x
9 in. x 5 in.)*

3 blocks of floral foam

*2 lengths of thin dowel
(approx. 5 in. each)*

Moss

8 peony foliage sprigs

*35 assorted summer (and
spring) blossoms in large,
medium, and small sizes*

With the splendor of a garden in full bloom and the vibrancy of a painter's palette, this playful summer arrangement proves too abundant for this small picnic hamper! We chose a collection of our favorite blossoms (1 or 2 from each color in the rainbow) and massed them inside this charming wicker case. It's a display that will brighten any room and enchant any visitor.

This is an easy arrangement to create because there are no difficult color decisions to make—you'll use them all! The flowers are placed close together to emphasize the "bursting" effect, so there's no need to reconstruct stems. Choose a similar selection of blossoms from your own garden to achieve the same colorful results.

1. Cut the blocks of floral foam to fit snugly inside the bottom portion of the wicker hamper. To keep the lid open, insert 2 lengths of dowel into the foam base toward the back of the hamper. Cover the foam with a layer of moss.

2. Insert the peony foliage into the moss-covered foam.

3. Assemble the large blossoms first. Glue them onto wires, and

spray them with surface sealers and colored floral sprays, if necessary. Evenly position them along the rim of the case and under the lid. We used 3 yellow sunflowers, 1 blue hydrangea, 3 asters (pink, white, and blue), 1 cream lily, and 1 white zinnia.

4. Next, assemble the medium-size flowers and glue them onto wires. Apply surface sealers and colored floral sprays, if necessary. Randomly insert the blossoms in the opening. We used 1 purple lilac, 1 white bishop's weed, 2 pink roses, 1 blue anemone, 2 red dahlias, and 1 yellow-orange dahlia.

5. To add depth to the arrangement, position the next layer of blossoms to extend slightly above the surrounding flowers. We used 4 green hellebore sprigs and 4 pink snapdragons.

6. Complete the arrangement by adding several small flowers. We used 5 yellow craspedia blossoms, 3 pink carnations, and 2 blue echinops.

GARDEN HARVEST

MATERIALS LIST

1 galvanized flower can (12 in. tall)

Floral foam

Spanish moss

6 dark blue delphinium

5 bells of Ireland

6 violet liatris

6 reconstructed peony stems (each with a single red flower)

30 Japanese iris leaves

2 reconstructed lily stems (with multiple cream or yellow flower heads)

Creating a fresh-flower arrangement begins with a trip to the garden, toting clippers and a galvanized flower can. We harvest flowers and foliage at their peak of perfection—cutting the stems long and casually placing them in the water-filled can. When the container is full of flowers, we retreat to the potting shed where we create our flower arrangements.

These forays to the flower garden inspired us to create a dried version of our summertime harvests. Beautifully preserved and loosely arranged, lilies, delphinium, liatris, peonies, and bells of Ireland fill our usually empty flower can during the long winter months. This casual gathering of flowers is well suited for a family room or a room with a garden theme.

1. Fill the galvanized flower can with a block of floral foam (the top of the foam block should be 3 in. to 4 in. below the rim). Lightly cover the surface with gray Spanish moss. Insert the delphinium stems into the foam base (the dark blue delphinium cultivar 'Black Knight' was our choice because it retains its color long after drying).

2. Apply 2 coats of green floral spray to the bells of Ireland. When they are dry, insert them into the foam base so that the taller stems are positioned toward the back of the can.

3. Apply lavender and green floral spray to the liatris flower spikes and stems, then insert them into the foam base.

4. Before reconstructing the peony stems, apply surface sealers and colored floral sprays to the foliage and flower heads. Reconstruct the stems following the instructions on pp. 61-63. Insert the stems randomly throughout the arrangement.

5. Next, apply green floral spray to the Japanese iris foliage, and insert it randomly throughout the arrangement, keeping the tallest leaves toward the center.

6. Finally, apply surface sealers to the stems and flower heads of the lilies, followed by colored floral sprays. Glue the flower heads onto the stems, then position these beautiful but fragile flowers front and center in the arrangement.

GIFT FROM THE GARDEN

MATERIALS LIST

Brown kraft paper (30 in. x 32 in.)

4 multibranched stems of fibigia

3 violet liatris

11 salal sprigs

10 rose beauty

10 russian statice

2 sprays of baby's breath

3 blue asters

3 cream snapdragons

1 pink peony

18 strands of raffia (approx. 26 in. long)

Throughout the summer months, your garden will produce an abundant supply of flowers. Why not share your harvest with a friend who also enjoys flower arranging? We gathered together a collection of dried flowers to create this "fresh from the florist" gift bouquet. In keeping with an earthy, garden theme, we wrapped the flowers in brown kraft paper and tied them with a simple raffia bow.

If you decide to vary the selection of flowers, make sure you include all the elements that make an interesting arrangement: focal-point flowers, foliage, filler and line materials, and accent flowers. Once you gather, dry, and prepare a beautiful selection of garden flowers, all that is left for your friend is the fun part—arranging!

1. ♦ Prepare the flowers and foliage before you assemble the bouquet. Glue each flower head onto a wire or surrogate stem, then apply surface sealers and colored floral sprays. Cut the sheet of brown kraft paper to size, and fold over 2 diagonal corners to form a narrow kite shape (approximately 20 in. at its widest point). Begin assembling the bouquet with fibigia and liatris, which have long, stiff stems to give the bouquet support. Position the center liatris slightly higher than the other two.

2. ♦ Layer the remaining materials on top of each other, staggering the position of

each flower and foliage sprig as it's placed. On top of the fibigia and liatris, lay in 3 salal sprigs, followed by 3 rose beauty, 4 Russian statice, I spray of baby's breath, and 2 more sprigs of salal.

3. ♦ Continue the layering with 2 asters, I snapdragon, 5 rose beauty, 4 Russian statice, I pink peony, and 2 sprigs of salal.

4. ♦ For the final layer, position I spray of baby's breath, 2 snapdragons, 2 Russian statice, 2 rose beauty, and I aster.

5. Once the layers are complete, conceal the stems beneath 4 sprigs of salal. Because this foliage is positioned low on the bouquet, it may be necessary to bend the wire stems in half so the wires are even with the cut ends of the fibigia and liatris stems.

6. To complete the gift, first fold over the tip of the "kite's" tail about 2 in. Then fold over the rest of the tail to cover the bottom of the stems. Gently curl the sides of the paper around the bouquet. The paper is stiff and will have a tendency to spring back open, so spot-glue the sides to the tail. For extra protection, wrap the bouquet and paper sleeve in a sheet of cellophane. Finish your gift with a simple raffia bow.

Chapter 6

Fall Arrangements

Golden sunflowers, russet leaves, and orange pumpkins are hallmark ingredients of autumn arrangements. Combine them with other warm-hued flowers and seedpods to create beautiful harvest-time displays.

Sunflower

Sunflower

Pumpkin Vase

AUTUMN PUMPKIN VASE

A vase crafted from a freshly picked pumpkin is the perfect container for a casual gathering of bright sunflowers and marigolds. To produce a fresh and lively appearance, this arrangement also contains money plant, foxtail millet, and scarlet-seeded iris pods. Their graceful curved stems mimic the loose casual nature of fresh flowers and alleviate the stiff, contrived look that plagues many dried-flower arrangements.

Plan to make this arrangement for a special event—the dried flowers will last longer than the container! When the pumpkin vase withers after several days, remove the arrangement and place it in a non-perishable container or carefully store it in a box for use the following year.

1.♦ For the vase, choose a well-rounded pumpkin with a fairly broad base. Cut the top off the pumpkin as you would for a jack-o'-lantern, and scoop out the pulp and seeds (if you carve a face, line the openings with moss). Find a plastic container that fits snugly inside the pumpkin (we use a plastic flowerpot). Place the rim of the container even with the rim of the pumpkin. If necessary, shim or wedge the container with cutoff pieces of floral foam. Fill the container with foam and cover it with moss.

2.♦ Glue a length of 21-gauge wire onto the back of each lady's mantle leaf, then lightly spray each leaf and each sprig of money plant with green floral spray. Insert the money plant into the foam first, then fill in any gaps with the lady's mantle leaves. Position some of the leaves so they drape over the rim.

3.♦ Spray each marigold with surface sealers, and glue them onto wires. Nestle the flowers into the greens to create depth in the arrangement and to help conceal their wire stems.

4. ♦ Once the marigolds are in place, insert the scarlet-seeded iris pods. Evenly distribute them throughout the arrangement, and position the pods to extend just beyond the greens.

5. ♦ Next, lightly spray each sunflower with surface sealers. Position them in the arrangement so they radiate from the center and are evenly spaced as you view the composition from all sides. Like the iris pods, the sunflowers should extend just beyond the greens.

6. ♦ Add foxtail millet as the final ingredient in the pumpkin vase. Insert the stems so they radiate from the center of the arrangement and the seed heads extend just beyond the flowers, pods, and greenery.

OCTOBER HARVEST

Showcase your mini-pumpkins or small gourds in this harvest arrangement. Combining them with dried flowers in a range of deep, rich hues makes this floral design perfect for welcoming your guests during the fall holidays.

Circular shapes are a repeating theme throughout this composition. We started with a round container and added pumpkins, dahlias, and marigolds. To add variety, we added spiny safflower buds, larkspur, and draping amaranth panicles.

Typically, mini-pumpkins last for months, but to incorporate them into this arrangement, their rinds must be punctured with wooden picks. Puncturing the rind speeds the decaying process, so the pumpkins may need to be replaced if you want the arrangement to last more than a month.

1. If you are using a wire container as your vase, first line the vessel with moss so the floral foam will not show through the bottom and sides. Fill the vase with floral foam, securing it to the vase with wires. Conceal the foam beneath a layer of moss. Using safflower buds as a foliage substitute along with lady's mantle leaves, glue them onto 21-gauge wires. Spray the buds and leaves with green floral spray, then arrange them so they radiate from the center of the container and form a rounded dome.

2. Nestle sprigs of blue statice into the greenery as shown in the photo. Insert a wooden pick into the bottom of each mini-pumpkin or small gourd. If your picks are too short to give the height you need, use lengths of ¼-in. dowel or the sturdy cut-off stem ends of other dried materials (we made our own picks out of dried echinacea and money plant stems). Position the pumpkins evenly to follow the shape of the greenery.

3. Next, position the red dahlias. In their fresh state, these dahlias were fire-engine red, but they turned a beautiful deep maroon when dried in silica gel. Spray them with sealers and a light application of burgundy floral spray to enhance their natural color. Glue the flower heads onto wires (the rounded shape of the arrangement will conceal the wire stems). Evenly place them throughout the arrangement.

4. Treat the marigolds and apricot dahlias in a similar way to the red dahlias—by gluing the flower heads onto wires and applying surface sealers. The vibrant colors of the dried marigolds and apricot dahlias do not require an application of colored floral sprays. Position the flowers randomly throughout the arrangement to complete the mounded shape.

5. Before you insert the amaranth panicles, apply green floral spray and extend their stems with wire and tape, if necessary. Position the majority of blooms at the rim of the container so they drape over the edges. Add a few near the top of the arrangement so they cascade over the flowers.

6. Finish the composition with lilac larkspur. Position the stems so they radiate from the center of the arrangement and extend slightly above the other plant materials.

INDIAN SUMMER

MATERIALS LIST

Floral foam (2 in. x 3 in. x 4 in.)

Moss

14 oats

4 orach sprigs

7 blue larkspur

Lavender-blue ribbon (2 yd.)

Olive-green ribbon (2 yd.)

6 salal sprigs

1 small terra-cotta flowerpot

3 bishop's weed flower heads

6 small curly willow twigs

1 yellow rose

2 yellow-orange lilies

5 colorful fall leaves

Reminiscent of warm Indian-summer days, when nature gives us one final glimpse of summer, this swag echoes the seasonal transition into autumn. Like the change of seasons, contrast is a repeating theme throughout this composition. Juxtaposing warm and cool colors, as well as rustic and refined materials, gives this swag a seasonally appropriate look with a touch of elegance.

The choice of contrasting colors was the first step in the design process—warm yellows and oranges combined with cool lavender-blue. Then we paired rustic fall materials, such as oats, orach, twigs, autumn leaves, and a terra-cotta pot, with elegant summer lilies, gossamer ribbons, and a rose. All the plant materials in this swag are naturally colored (with the exception of the salal leaves) and will fade gracefully over time.

1. ◆ Cut a 3-in. piece of wooden pick and an 18-in. length of 22-gauge wire. Wrap the center portion of the wire around the pick, then insert both wire ends into the block of foam until they protrude from the top of the block. Pull the wire ends until the pick sits firmly against the block, and twist the ends together to create a hanger. Cover the 5 exposed sides of the block with moss, securing it with greening pins. Hang the foam base on a wall.

3. ◆ Combine the 2 ribbon colors to create a simple bow with long loops and trailing ends (see the sidebar on p. 157). Secure the bow with wire, and insert the wire ends into the foam base. Next, position the salal sprigs so they radiate out from the bow: 4 long stems inserted below the bow and 2 smaller sprigs above (if necessary, glue in extra single leaves to fill in any gaps).

2. ◆ Using the photo as a guide for length, cut the stems of the oats, orach, and larkspur before they are inserted in the top and bottom of the foam block (the stems do not actually go all the way through the center of the foam). Insert the flower and seedhead portions of the stems into the bottom of the foam block, positioning them in a fan shape. Then insert the cut-off stem ends into the top of the foam block to mimic the stem ends of the materials below.

4. Next, attach the small terra-cotta pot. Cover a 9-in., 21-gauge wire with floral tape, and thread it through the hole in the bottom of the pot. Bend the wire ends perpendicular to the side of the pot, then apply glue to the ends of the wire and immediately insert them into the foam. Glue and tape the bishop's weed flower heads onto wires and insert them into the foam as shown in the photo. Randomly insert the curly willow twigs into the base.

6. Finally, attach the fall leaves. Start by inserting the stem of the largest leaf into the foam base, just below the pot. Tie a loose overhand knot at the end of each ribbon, then insert the stems of the remaining leaves into the knots and tighten. Finish with a decorative dovetail cut on the end of each ribbon.

5. Glue and tape the rose (we used a 'Peace' rose) and lily flowers onto wires. Next, glue a small piece of floral foam inside the

flowerpot and insert the rose. Fill any gaps between the rose and the pot rim with moss. Position the lilies as shown in the photo.

SEED POD TOPIARY

MATERIALS LIST

*1 square container (7 in. x
7 in. x 6 in.)*

Moss

Floral foam

*6 fresh, pliable branches (2 ft. to
3 ft. long)*

1 Styrofoam ball (5 in. dia.)

20 individual salal leaves

1 or 2 hop vines

2 large hydrangeas

8 echinacea seed heads

10 small pinecones

8 starflower seed heads

10 nigella pods

10 poppy pods

14 gold "berry" sprays

By late summer or early autumn your garden will be full of interesting seed pods. These pods hold the promise of future gardens. Save a few pods for seeds, but harvest the majority for decorative use in arrangements.

This easy-to-make topiary tree is a seed pod sampler. The collection of pods comes in a beautiful range of autumn colors including dark brown, light brown, buff-gray, green, and maroon. Hop flowers, hydrangea blossoms, and green salal leaves round out this small tree, making it a perfect fall decoration. To complete the autumn setting, display the topiary with organic items such as potted plants, gourds, or baskets of pinecones.

1. Line your container with moss if the foam will show, then cut and insert a block of floral foam. Create the topiary trunk by grouping 6 branches and binding them together with wire at the widest end. At the opposite end, separate the branches into 3 sets of 2 branches and braid them together. Once you've braid-

ed approximately 15 in., bind off the branches with wire. Trim the branches 1 in. above the second wire. Insert the widest end of the trunk into the foam base, and push the Styrofoam ball onto the top of the trunk. Using greening pins, secure moss to the ball and around the base of the trunk.

3. Cut your hop vines into 14 small sprigs that consist of 3 to 5 flowers each, and lightly spray them with green floral spray. Cut the hydrangea blossoms into 9 small clusters. We chose blue hydrangeas that turn a beautiful maroon color in autumn. If necessary, tape the hydrangea clusters and hop sprigs onto short lengths of wire. Position them evenly over the ball.

2. Glue a short length of 21-gauge wire to the back of each salal leaf, and apply a light coating of green floral spray. Insert the leaves evenly over the ball so they radiate from the center.

4. Next, cut the echinacea stems short, and insert them evenly over the ball. Wrap a length of 21-gauge wire around the base bracts of each pinecone, and insert the wire ends into the Styrofoam.

5. Insert a variety of pods to fill in the remaining gaps. We used starflower seed heads, nigella pods, and poppy pods. However, any dried seed pods or edible nuts will work as long as they blend with the scale and color scheme.

6. Finally, add the finishing touch of tiny gold "berries" to your topiary. They typically come in large clustered sprays and are available at craft stores. Cut the "berries" from their sprays (leaving their tiny wires attached), and tape them in clusters to short lengths of 21-gauge wire. Insert 14 "berry" clusters evenly over the topiary tree.

HARVEST WREATH

MATERIALS LIST

1 grapevine wreath form (18 in.)

6 or 7 salal sprigs

2 artificial pears

3 artificial plums

*2 artificial grape clusters
(1 large, 1 small)*

5 cardoon buds and blossoms

1 or 2 hop vines

9 small clusters of ageratum

14 small clusters of oregano

9 curly willow twigs

This wreath holds all the ingredients of a bountiful harvest. Flowers, herbs, and a delightful tangle of hop vines surround a collection of seemingly fresh-picked grapes, pears, and plums. Twisted, curly willow branches contribute to the "untamed" look, while the grapevine wreath adds to the harvest theme.

Most craft stores carry a selection of artificial fruits and vegetables, but some are more realistic than others. Do some searching and purchase the most realistic fruits you can find. They cost a bit more but the extra expense is worth it—their lifelike colors and details will make your arrangements come alive.

1. Determine the front and top of your wreath form. On the top and back of the wreath, create a hanger by attaching a small loop of wire to the vines. Hang the wreath form on a wall at a comfortable work height. Apply green floral spray to the salal sprigs, and attach them to the wreath with glue (reserve 1 salal sprig to use in step 2). Position them around the left side of the wreath form, following the curve, until they form a C shape.

2. Position the artificial fruits as shown in the photo, then use wires to attach the grapes and glue to secure the pears and plums. Glue the reserved salal leaves at the base of the pears and plums to visually anchor the fruit to the wreath.

3. Apply green floral spray to the back of each cardoon bud and flower and purple spray to the tuft in the flower's center. (To keep the purple floral spray directed on the center of the bloom, create a paper tube with the same diameter as the flower's center. Hold the tube over the flower and spray within it.) Glue 3 large cardoons (ascending in size) on the left side of the wreath, following the curve, then glue 2 smaller buds (ascending in size) on the bottom right of the wreath.

4. Cut the hop vines into approximately 11 sprigs, and glue them around the fruits and cardoons. Allow some sprigs to hang into the open center of the wreath.

5. Next, position the accent flowers, ageratum, and oregano. Lightly spray the ageratum with violet floral spray. Evenly distribute the flowers throughout the wreath and glue them in place.

6. To give the wreath a natural, "untamed" look, add a few curly willow twigs. Once you have determined their positions, glue them in place.

GARDEN CORNUCOPIA

MATERIALS LIST

1 cornucopia basket

1½ blocks of floral foam

Moss

15 money plant sprigs

1 artificial green apple

2 artificial pears

9 small peegee hydrangea blossoms

9 fall-colored maple leaves

13 oat sprigs

12 apricot statice sprigs

4 apricot dahlias

Hunter-green, russet-brown, and pumpkin-orange are the traditional colors of fall. If this palette is a bit too dark for your taste, consider their elegant tints—celadon-green, salmon-pink, and apricot. These colors are found in a variety of materials including oats, seed pods, fruits, flowers, and colorful leaves. This combination, spilling from a cornucopia basket, still says fall but with a softer voice.

We collected fall leaves in a variety of colors for our garden cornucopia. While it's possible to air-dry autumn leaves between newspaper sections, we prefer to dry them in silica gel to prevent wrinkling. It's always a pleasant surprise when they are removed from the crystals—the once vividly colored leaves emerge with softer, muted shades.

1. Fill the cavity of the basket with floral foam, then position the full block of foam on the bottom of the basket. Shape the block with a knife, and secure it in place with wires or glue. Next, shape the half block to sit snuggly on top of the full block, and glue it in place. Cut the protruding ends of the blocks flush with the basket opening, and cover the foam with moss. Apply green floral spray to the money plant sprigs, and position them as shown in the photo.

3. Choose 9 small hydrangea blossoms or cut 1 or 2 large flower heads into smaller clusters. Lengthen their stems if necessary with tape and wire, and insert the flowers as shown in the photo. The peegee hydrangeas we used in this arrangement were dried in silica gel during the summer to capture their creamy white color.

2. Position the apple and pears next, starting by inserting the pointed end of a wooden pick into the bottom of each piece of artificial fruit. Remove the thin wire and insert the blunt end of the pick into the foam base. Arrange the apple and pears so their positions radiate from the center of the basket.

4. ♦ Spray the collection of fall leaves with a surface sealer. Position the leaves and oats evenly throughout the arrangement so they radiate from the center of the composition.

5. ♦ Tuck in sprigs of apricot statice around the fruits. Also use them to fill in any gaps in the arrangement.

6. ♦ Finally, nestle 4 dahlia blossoms around the fruit. We applied surface sealers to our silica-dried dahlias but did not apply colored floral sprays. If necessary, glue wire stems to the flower heads.

Chapter 7

Winter Arrangements

Envision snowy-white lilies gracing a deep green holly wreath or Christmas tree ornaments made with jewel-toned flowers; these are just a few combinations perfect for holiday decorating.

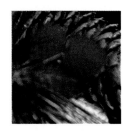

RUSTIC HOLIDAYS

With all the charm of a lakeside cabin, this whimsical winter arrangement harbors a small green canoe as its focal point. Twigs, pinecones, and a woven willow basket give this composition a rustic theme. To herald the approaching holidays, we included a single red candle, white dahlias, and rich, green pine boughs. For safety, always be in attendance when the candle is lit.

We used a combination of artificial and air-dried evergreen boughs in this arrangement. The artificial pine was purchased at a craft store and the fresh noble fir from a local florist shop. Most fresh evergreen branches shed their needles when dried; however, noble fir needles (air-dried at room temperature) stay firmly attached for months. If noble fir is not available in your area, purchase artificial boughs with a similar look.

1. Fill the basket with floral foam, and secure it with glue or wires. Determine the canoe's location, then glue a small piece of foam toward the back of the foam base so the canoe sits at a sloping angle. Determine the candle's location, and insert a candleholder into the foam base. Next, conceal the foam with moss, and insert the candle into the holder. After positioning the canoe, insert a wooden pick deep into the foam base between the candle and the side of the canoe. Secure the canoe in place by wrapping the pick's thin wire around the nearest crossbrace inside the canoe.

3. Spray the noble fir branches with a sealer and green floral spray, then insert them between the artificial pine branches to fill in the gaps. Wrap a 21-gauge wire around the base bracts of each pinecone to create a pick (or attach them to wooden picks). Position the pinecones among the branches as shown in the photo.

2. Insert the artificial pine boughs (ours came with a single cone attached to each branch), positioning the branches so they radiate from the center of the arrangement. Insert one sprig near the bow of the canoe to slightly tip the canoe at an angle toward the candle.

4. Now, add the line materials. We used the stems of air-dried scotch broom and colored them with green floral spray. Position the scotch broom behind and to the left of the candle, then insert the 3 long curly willow twigs among the scotch broom. (For safety: Make sure these tall line materials are positioned several inches away from the candle; always be in attendance when the candle is lit; and never allow the candle to burn down completely.) Insert the 7 small curly willow twigs randomly among the evergreen branches to enhance the rustic, untamed look.

5. Next, prepare the silica-dried bishop's weed and white pompon dahlias, which are the bright spots in this arrangement. Tape the flower heads onto 21-gauge wires and spray them with surface sealers. Position the largest bishop's weed flower at the base of the candle and the 2 smaller ones as shown in the photo. Insert the white dahlias randomly among the branches and cones.

6. Finally, lightly spray the gomphrena with red floral spray. Divide the 15 stems into groups of 3 and tape them together. Insert the 5 groups of gomphrena as shown in the photo to add bright red color spots. Fill in any remaining gaps with small sprigs of baby's breath.

WINTER-WHITE WREATH

MATERIALS LIST

Heavy-duty gloves

1 wire wreath form (20 in.)

60 fresh holly sprigs (berries removed)

Celadon ribbon (3 yd. x 2½ in.)

5 white lilies

10 small peegee hydrangeas

12 white pompon dahlias

13 bishop's weed flower heads

28 small baby's breath sprigs

The elegance of winter-white flowers set against a deep green holly wreath is reminiscent of snow-covered branches in early winter. This classic holiday wreath is striking yet subtle enough to blend with almost any home decor or color scheme.

If you are planning to hang this wreath for a special holiday gathering, make the fresh holly wreath base 6 to 8 weeks ahead of time. The thick leaves and stems need plenty of time to dry at room temperature (drying times vary with temperature and humidity). If you are fortunate enough to have a holly tree in your backyard, harvest the branches in early autumn. Otherwise, purchase fresh holly branches from a florist or garden center.

1. Beginning with a wire wreath form, fresh holly sprigs, and a paddle of 22-gauge wire, attach one end of the wire to the wreath form. Position 3 holly sprigs over the wreath form, and secure them by tightly wrapping the wire around the stems and form. Overlap the first group of holly with an additional 3 sprigs and wire those to the form. Continue until the form is covered with holly sprigs. Using a small length of wire, create a hanger on the back of the wreath. Dry the wreath in a well-ventilated room. Once the holly is dry, spray the leaves with green floral spray.

2. Create a simple ribbon bow with 25-in.-long tails (see the sidebar on p. 157). We used wire-edged ribbon because it is easy to manipulate and holds its shape. Wire the bow to the top of the wreath, and tuck the long tails into the leaves as shown in the photo.

3. Next, spray the silica-dried lilies with surface sealers. Arrange them on the top portion of the wreath, and glue them in place.

4. Select 10 small hydrangea blossoms or cut 1 or 2 large flower heads into smaller clusters. The peegee hydrangeas used in this wreath were dried in silica gel during the summer to capture their creamy white color. Position the blossoms randomly around the wreath, and glue them in place.

5. Position the white pompon dahlias and bishop's weed flowers next. Randomly place them throughout the holly leaves until the surface of the wreath is covered by an even distribution of flowers, then glue them in place.

6. To complete the wreath's winter-white theme, add baby's breath. Work your way around the wreath, tucking small sprigs into any open gaps.

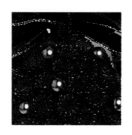

NATURE'S ORNAMENTS

MATERIALS LIST

Styrofoam balls (2½ in. dia.)

Assorted flower heads (approx. 60 to 80 per flower ornament)

Assorted "berry" sprays or small glass ornaments (approx. 20 to 25 per flower ornament)

Assorted ribbons

Since Christmas ornaments are hidden away for most of the year, it's an exciting day when the boxes containing them are finally opened. These colorful decorations reflect the holiday lights and instantly brighten a room. With a bit of springtime planning, it's possible to grow your own Christmas-tree ornaments. These flower ornaments are easy to make and will last for several holiday seasons. A variety of flowers are suitable for this project, including ammobium, hops, strawflowers, bells of Ireland, larkspur, craspedia, and our durable favorite—gomphrena. (Ornaments made with delicate-petaled flowers, such as hops, may only last one season.)

Creating homegrown holiday decoration can be a fun family tradition. The bells of Ireland ornaments do not require a hot-glue gun, making them a perfect project for children.

1. Insert a 4-in. to 5-in. length of 21-gauge wire through the center of a Styrofoam ball, and bend a small hook in one end. Continue pulling the wire until the hook end is flush with the bottom of the ball. Shorten the protruding end of wire if necessary, and bend it over to create a loop for hanging the ornament on a Christmas tree.

2. Remove the flower heads from their stems (in this case gomphrena), and glue them onto the ball. Place them close together so the Styrofoam doesn't show. If you are adding small glass ornaments (as shown), glue them on as you glue on the flower heads. First remove the small wire hanger from each glass ornament, then place a drop of glue on the neck of the ornament and insert it into the Styrofoam.

3. To add small beadlike ornaments, start with wired "berry" sprays (available at craft stores). Completely cover the Styrofoam ball with flower heads. Then cut the individual "berries" off the sprays, leaving their short lengths of wire attached. Insert the wire into the Styrofoam so the beadlike ornaments sit snuggly against the flower heads.

4. To make an ornament from bells of Ireland, begin by spray-painting a complete flower stem gold. Once the paint is dry, use scissors to snip off the individual "bells" just above the seeds in their centers, creating a hole at the base of each bell. Cut red, wired "berries" off their spray, and insert one into the center of each "bell" so the wire protrudes through the hole. Push the wire into the Styrofoam ball. Repeat this process until the Styrofoam ball is completely covered.

5. As a finishing touch, attach color-coordinated bows. First make the bows and attach them to wires, then insert the wires into the Styrofoam near the wire loops.

To hang your new ornaments on a Christmas tree, attach a standard ornament hook to each wire loop.

HOW TO MAKE A BOW

The following instructions show how to make a simplified florist bow using double-faced ribbon. If your ribbon has a right and wrong side, make a full twist in the ribbon (between your thumb and forefinger) each time you make a loop so the right side always faces outward.

1. Make a small center loop, and pinch the crossover between your thumb and forefinger.

3. Make a long loop to the right and pinch. (Repeat steps 2 and 3 to create a bow with multiple loops.)

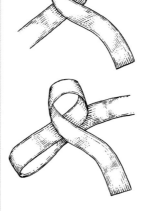

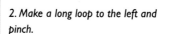

2. Make a long loop to the left and pinch.

4. Secure the bow by slipping a wire through the center loop and twisting the ends together. For a finishing touch, make decorative dovetail cuts on the ribbon ends.

HOLIDAY HYDRANGEA
GARLAND

MATERIALS LIST

*1 artificial evergreen garland
(6 ft.)*

2 large pinecones

18 holly sprigs (berries removed)

4 large hydrangeas

Blue ribbon (5 yd. x 2½ in.)

6 echinops

40 dusty miller leaves

*11 silver ornaments
(1½ in. dia.)*

9 silver ornaments (1 in. dia.)

Create an elegant holiday atmosphere with this winter hydrangea garland. The combination of greenery, silver ornaments, winter-blue flowers, and shimmering ribbon makes a perfect winter decoration for draping over a mirror, mantle, or staircase balustrade.

Hydrangeas are the focal-point flowers of this garland. Their large size makes them a wonderful flower to work with because they cover a lot of area very quickly (a plus during the busy holiday season). The basic evergreen garland is made from imitation spruce branches. The garland's blue-green color harmonizes perfectly with the blue hydrangeas and echinops. We also included dried holly sprigs to help carry the holiday theme and offset the garland's artificial appearance. And finally, we added shimmering blue ribbon and reflective silver ornaments to catch the sparkle of holiday lights.

1. For best results, hang your bare garland in its final position and decorate it in place. Bend and position the individual evergreen sprigs until the garland has a full and fluffy appearance. Attach a large pinecone to each end of the garland by wrapping a length of wire around the bracts at the base of each cone and then twisting the wire around the end of the garland.

3. Next, apply 2 or 3 different shades of blue and purple floral sprays to the 4 hydrangeas. Cut the hydrangea blossoms into approximately 5 clusters each, for a total of about 20 flower clusters. Stagger the clusters along the garland, and secure them in place with glue.

2. Apply green floral spray to each sprig of holly. Stagger their positions along the garland, and glue them in place.

4. Once the hydrangeas are positioned, wind the ribbon throughout the garland. We used wire-edged ribbon because it's easy to manipulate and holds its shape. Begin at one end and slowly work your way along the garland. Tuck the ribbon in and around the sprigs and flowers (the ribbon is not actually wound around the garland). Finish by making a decorative dovetail cut at each end of the ribbon.

5. Add the blue echinops and silver-gray dusty miller leaves, which are the accent materials. If necessary, lightly spray the echinops with blue floral spray. Create 13 clusters of dusty miller leaves by taping groups of 3 or 4 leaves onto single 21-gauge wires. Position the echinops and dusty miller clusters along the garland, and use them to fill in any bare spots. Secure the materials in place with glue.

6. Nestle the silver ornaments around the flowers and foliage. Randomly position them throughout the garland, and glue them in place.

WINTER GATHERING

MATERIALS LIST

1 vase (10 in. tall)

Floral foam

Moss

5 eucalyptus branches

3 scotch broom branches

6 small nobel fir branches

6 pinecones (2 large, 4 small)

30 dusty miller leaves

5 echinops

5 poppy pods

1 blue aster

T all and slender in stature, the sweeping lines of this arrangement will add a touch of formal elegance to your home. Gathered from a winter garden, evergreen boughs and pinecones form the base of this arrangement, while eucalyptus and scotch broom establish the lines. Flowers, seed pods, and foliage in silver-gray and cerulean blue complete the winter theme.

To create the flowing lines of this arrangement, choose eucalyptus and scotch broom branches that have naturally curved stems (preserve them with glycerin to keep the stems flexible). Once they are placed in the arrangement, you can fine-tune the direction of their curves by wrapping thin wires around the stems and gently bending them in the desired direction (the thin wires removed from wooden picks work well).

1. ◆ Insert a piece of floral foam into the neck of your vase so it extends about 1 in. to 1½ in. above the rim. Cover it with moss. Next, position the eucalyptus and scotch broom to establish the flowing lines of your arrangement, inserting them as shown in the photo.

2. ◆ Spray the small noble fir branches with a surface sealer and green floral spray, then position them as shown in the photo so they radiate from the center of the arrangement. We used air-dried, noble fir branches in this design because they hold their needles well. If noble fir is not available in your area, use artificial evergreen branches.

3. ◆ Wrap a length of 21-gauge wire around the base bracts of each cone. To position the highest cone, tape its wire to a sturdy, thin, 10-in. stick (we used a dried echinacea stem). Insert the cones as shown in the photo with the 2 large cones placed on either side of the vase rim and pointing in the direction of the line materials.

4. ♦ Next, add the dusty miller leaves to lighten this otherwise dark arrangement. Tape the leaves in groups of 3 onto 21-gauge wires, creating 10 clusters. Position them in and around the cones and greenery to fill in any gaps.

5. ♦ Lightly spray the echinops with blue floral spray. Position the echinops and poppy pods so they radiate from the center of the arrangement and point in the direction of the lines established by the eucalyptus, scotch broom, and fir branches.

6. ♦ Finally, add the large, perfectly shaped aster as the focal point of this arrangement. All the surrounding materials radiate outward from this single blossom. Glue the silica-dried aster onto a wire, then apply surface sealers and a touch of blue floral spray. Position the blossom in the center of the composition near the vase rim and between the 2 large cones.

WINTER POTPOURRI

MATERIALS LIST

Round silver container (3½ in. x 6½ in. dia.)

Floral foam

Moss

11 salal sprigs

6 bishop's weed

2 or 3 large hydrangeas

9 red-crested celosia

6 blue asters, including stems

33 dusty miller leaves

11 ageratum sprigs

19 lilac larkspur

21 purple gomphrena

The wide range of shapes, colors, and textures in this sumptuous gathering of flowers reminds us of floral potpourri—and provides a welcome respite from winter's chill. An assortment of soft flowers and velvety foliage mingle together in a silver container to create a subtle, formal ambiance. The symmetry of this arrangement further strengthens the appeal and formality of this colorful design.

This harmonious color scheme combines the deep, wintry hues of blue, magenta, and burgundy. To brighten the selection of flowers we used small groups of silver-gray dusty miller leaves. Their texture matched the velvety celosia and soft ageratum, while the finely cut shape of their leaves repeated the filigree pattern in the container.

1. ♦ Begin by lining the sides of your container with moss if the foam will show. Fill the container with floral foam, and cover it with moss. Spray the salal sprigs with green floral spray, and tape the bishop's weed flower heads onto wires. Next, insert the salal sprigs so they create a loose mound shape. Nestle the bishop's weed into the sprigs to create depth in the arrangement and to help conceal their wire stems.

3. ♦ Insert the rich, velvety celosia blooms next. If necessary, brighten the flowers with a light application of a burgundy-red floral spray. Evenly distribute them throughout the arrangement so they follow the rounded shape established by the foliage.

2. ♦ Apply 2 or 3 different shades of blue and purple floral spray to the hydrangeas. Cut the blossoms into 9 smaller clusters, and tape them onto 21-gauge wires. Position them so they extend above the bishop's weed but not beyond the outermost leaf tips.

4. For a fresh appearance, reconstruct entire aster stems (see pp. 61-63 for details). Insert the asters into the arrangement so they extend just beyond the hydrangeas and celosia.

5. Tape clusters of 2 or 3 dusty miller leaves onto 21-gauge wires, and lightly spray the ageratum flowers with lavender floral spray. Position both flowers randomly throughout the arrangement so they extend just beyond the asters.

6. Insert larkspur flower spikes so they radiate from the center of the arrangement and extend just beyond the other materials in the composition. Fill in any remaining gaps with groups of 2 or 3 gomphrena blossoms.

PART THREE

flowers for all seasons:
A PLANT GUIDE

ACHILLEA
Yarrow
Perennial

＞＋＊＞－○－＜＊＋＜

Color Pink, rose, red, orange, apricot, yellow, purple
Height 6 in. – 48 in.
Spacing 12 in.
Sowing Depth Surface-sow
Germination Temp 65°F – 75°F
Germination Time 7 – 14 days

Yarrow plants readily start from seed; grow and spread rapidly; are happy in average garden soil; and resist drought. *Achillea filipendulina* is topped with large, golden-yellow flower heads. They air-dry easily, retaining their color and form. *Achillea millefolium* (shown above) comes in a wide range of colors. The individual florets tend to shrink during the drying process, so use this species as a filler flower.

Growing About 4 to 6 weeks before the last frost, fill a flat with soilless mix. Sow the seeds on the surface, but do not cover them with additional medium. Once the seeds have germinated and the seedlings are large enough to handle, transplant them to cell flats. After all danger of frost has passed, transplant them to a sunny location in the garden.

Harvesting Harvest the flowers when they are in full bloom. Cut the stems long for use in large arrangements; they can always be trimmed for a particular project.

Drying Bundle several stems together with a rubber band and hang them upside down to dry.

AGERATUM HOUSTONIANUM
Flossflower
Annual

＞＋＊＞－○－＜＊＋＜

Color Wine-red, lavender-blue, white
Height 6 in. – 30 in.
Spacing 9 in. – 12 in.
Sowing Depth Surface-sow
Germination Temp 75°F – 80°F
Germination Time 5 – 10 days

Ageratum is usually grown as a bedding plant, but several cultivars including 'Blue Horizon' and 'Red Top' have long stems that are perfect for flower arranging. Even though their fuzzy blooms shrink during the drying process, they still remain attractive and colorful. Tuck *Ageratum* into small- and medium-size arrangements for subtle color spots and added texture.

Growing About 6 to 7 weeks before the last frost, fill a seed flat with soilless mix and sow the seeds on the surface. Once they've germinated and the seedlings are large enough to handle, transplant them to cell flats. After all danger of frost has passed, transplant them to a sunny location in the garden.

Harvesting Harvest *Ageratum* when they are in full bloom but before the fuzzy flowers begin to lighten and wither.

Drying Bundle several stems together with a rubber band and hang them upside down to dry. Apply a surface sealer and colored floral sprays to the dried blooms and stems.

ALCEA ROSEA
Hollyhock
Annual/Biennial/Short-Lived Perennial

>⊢◆>⊶○⊷◀⊣<

Color Pink, rose, red, peach, apricot, yellow, white
Height 24 in. – 96 in.
Spacing 12 in. – 14 in.
Sowing Depth ⅛ in.
Germination Temp 65°F – 70°F
Germination Time 10 – 14 days

The addition of hollyhocks will quickly turn the look of your dried flower garden into a cottage garden. These old-fashioned flowers come in tall and dwarf varieties with either double or single blooms. Use individual dried blossoms on wreaths and garlands, or dry and reconstruct stems for use in arrangements.

Growing About 6 to 8 weeks before the last frost, sow the seeds in a soilless mix. Once they've germinated and the seedlings are large enough to handle, transplant them to cell flats. After all danger of frost has passed, transplant them to a garden location with full sun and well-drained soil. Hollyhocks may require staking in windy areas.

Harvesting Cut the flowers from their stems when they are in full bloom. If you plan to reconstruct a stem (see pp. 61-63), harvest buds and flowers at various stages of development. Harvest the mature stems in late summer.

Drying Place the blossoms, buds, and stems in a container of silica gel and cover with additional silica gel. Once dry, apply a spray sealer and colored floral sprays.

ALCHEMILLA MOLLIS
Lady's Mantle
Perennial

>⊢◆>⊶○⊷◀⊣<

Color Yellow-green
Height 20 in.
Spacing 16 in. – 18 in.
Sowing Depth Surface-sow
Germination Temp 65°F – 70°F
Germination Time 20 – 30 days

Lady's mantle has frothy sprays of tiny yellow-green flowers that look just as pleasing spilling onto a path as they do tucked into a summer arrangement. In the garden, the fuzzy hairs on each leaf capture small droplets of dew-like clear liquid mercury. Both the flowers and leaves dry easily.

Growing In early spring, sow the seeds in a soilless mix, but do not cover them with additional medium. Once they've germinated and the seedlings are large enough to handle, transplant them to cell flats. After all danger of frost has passed, transplant them to a sunny or semi shaded (in hot regions) area of the garden. These easy-to-grow perennials readily self-seed.

Harvesting Harvest lady's mantle when its tiny flowers are in full bloom. As the flowers mature, their color darkens. If picked too late, they will turn an unattractive brown as they dry. Harvest the leaves in midsummer.

Drying Bundle several stems together with a rubber band and hang them upside down to dry. Dry the leaves between newspaper sections or in silica gel.

AMARANTHUS
Amaranth
Annual

>─┤◆─○─◆├─<

Color Red, burgundy, green
Height 12 in. – 60 in.
Spacing 12 in. – 15 in.
Sowing Depth ¹⁄₁₆ in.
Germination Temp 70°F – 75°F
Germination Time 7 – 10 days

Amaranth flowers are either long, drooping panicles or upright spikes. Love-lies-bleeding (*Amaranthus caudatus*) is the most popular with its red, chenille-like blooms. Similar in form is 'Green Tails' with yellow-green blooms. 'Pygmy Torch' and 'Green Thumb' (*Amaranthus hypochondriacus*) produce 12-in. to 18-in., red and green flower spikes respectively. And for large arrangements, 'Prince's Feather' (*Amaranthus cruentus*) grows to an impressive 4 ft. to 5 ft. tall, bearing large, burgundy flower spikes.

Growing Plant the seeds in a soilless mix 6 to 7 weeks before the last frost date. Lightly cover the seeds with additional medium, then water them carefully to avoid burying the seeds. When the seedlings are large enough to handle, transplant them to individual cell flats. Once all danger of frost has passed, transplant them to a sunny position in the garden.

Harvesting Harvest the flowers when they are fully developed. If they are picked too early, the stems will shrivel.

Drying Hang the blooms upside down (either individually or in small bundles) in a warm location to ensure that their thick stems dry completely.

AMMI
Bishop's Weed
Annual

>─┤◆─○─◆├─<

Color White
Height 36 in. – 60 in.
Spacing 9 in. – 12 in.
Sowing Depth ¹⁄₁₆ in.
Germination Temp 60°F – 65°F
Germination Time 10 – 15 days

Lending a light and airy feel to arrangements, *Ammi majus* (shown above) is a Queen Anne's Lace look-alike. It air-dries easily and is used to great effect as a delicate filler flower. *Ammi visagna* has compact flower heads and blooms several weeks later.

Growing Prior to sowing, prechill the seed packets in the refrigerator for 1 to 2 weeks. Sow the seeds in a soilless mix, and lightly cover them with additional medium. When the seedlings are large enough to handle, transplant them to cell flats. After all danger of frost has passed, transplant them to a sunny location in the garden. Staking may be necessary to keep these tall plants from toppling.

Harvesting Harvest flowers in full bloom. If air-drying the flowers, leave 8 in. to 12 in. of stem attached to the head. Leave only 1 in. of stem attached if you plan to dry the flowers in silica gel. Air-dry several stems to recombine with the silica-dried flower heads.

Drying Air-dry *Ammi majus* using the drying rack described on pp. 39-40. Alternately, dry *Ammi majus* or *Ammi visagna* in silica gel to retain their natural form. Place the flower heads face up in a container of silica gel and cover them with additional silica gel. Once the flower heads dry, glue them onto wires or air-dried stems (see pp. 61-63).

AMMOBIUM ALATUM
Winged Everlasting
Annual

>-+-<>-0-<+-<

Color White
Height 24 in. – 36 in.
Spacing 10 in. – 12 in.
Sowing Depth 1/16 in.
Germination Temp 65°F – 70°F
Germination Time 10 – 15 days

Small, papery white flowers top the long stems of *Ammobium*. The petals (bracts) open to reveal bright yellow centers. The stems have thin protruding edges that give rise to its name "winged" everlasting. *Ammobium* is usually grown as an annual, but technically it's a tender perennial.

Growing About 6 to 8 weeks before the last frost, sow the seeds in a soilless mix. Once they've germinated, transplant the seedlings to cell flats and keep them there until all danger of frost has passed. *Ammobium* grows best in full sun and free-draining soil.

Harvesting Harvest the individual stems as the flowers begin to open and show a hint of yellow; the flowers will continue to open as they dry. If the flowers are picked too late, the centers will dry to an unattractive brown.

Drying Bundle several stems together with a rubber band and hang them upside down to dry. As the stems dry, they shrivel and are rarely strong enough to hold up the flower heads in humid conditions. Use adjacent flowers in your arrangements to support the *Ammobium* blooms or attach small clusters of the diminutive flowers to a wire or pick.

ANEMONE CORONARIA
Anemone
Tuberous-Rooted Perennial

>-+-<>-0-<+-<

Color Red, purple, rosy-purple, white
Height 8 in. – 15 in.
Spacing 8 in. – 12 in.
Planting Depth 1 in. – 2 in.
Plant Time See below
Harvest Time Spring and summer

Always grow enough anemones to enjoy in both fresh and dried arrangements. We grow two of the most well-known anemones: the De Caen hybrids (single blossoms) and the St. Brigid hybrids (double blossoms).

Growing Before planting, soak the tubers overnight in warm water. In Zones 7 to 9, plant the tubers in October or November. In Zones 4 to 6, plant them in the fall with a heavy winter mulch or plant them in the spring. In Zones 2 to 3, plant them in the spring after all danger of frost has passed. The oddly shaped tuber has a top and bottom. The side that faces up is typically rounded and has a depressed scar left by the previous year's growth.

Harvesting Cut the flower head off its stem when in full bloom.

Drying Place the flower heads face up in a container of silica gel and cover with additional silica gel. The flower petals are very thin and fragile. Once dry, spray them with several light coats of sealer; the applications must be light to prevent excessive curling. Hot-glue the flower heads onto wires or surrogate stems (see pp. 61-63).

ANTIRRHINUM MAJUS
Snapdragon
Annual

⊱⊶⊷⊙⊶⊷⊰

Color Pink, rose, red, orange, yellow, white
Height 8 in. – 36 in.
Spacing 9 in. – 12 in.
Sowing Depth Surface-sow
Germination Temp 65°F – 70°F
Germination Time 7 – 14 days

Snapdragons have a cottage garden ambiance and are beautiful in both fresh and dried arrangements. This old-time favorite dries well in silica gel and comes in a wide range of colors.

Growing Prior to sowing, prechill the seed packet in the refrigerator for 1 to 2 weeks. Approximately 8 weeks before the last frost, fill a seed flat with soilless mix and sow the seeds on the surface. Once they've germinated and the seedlings are large enough to handle, transplant them to cell flats. After all danger of frost has passed, transplant the seedlings to a sunny location in the garden.

Harvesting Harvest the flower spikes when the majority of florets are in full bloom. Remove any withering florets or developing seedpods from the bottom of the stem.

Drying Cut the stems to fit the length of your silica gel container. Lay each flower spike on its side and cover it with additional silica gel. When the flowers are dry, use a small paintbrush to whisk off residual silica gel. Apply a spray sealer to protect the flowers and stems.

ATRIPLEX HORTENSIS
Orach
Annual

⊱⊶⊷⊙⊶⊷⊰

Color Red, buff-yellow, green
Height 48 in. – 72 in.
Spacing 18 in. – 24 in.
Sowing Depth 1/16 in.
Germination Temp 60°F – 65°F
Germination Time 7 – 10 days

Orach is a tall, branching plant that is best suited for the back of a border. By late summer, its long stems are covered with hundreds of small, flat seedpods. The leaves, stems, and pods of 'Cupreata' have a deep, wine-red color and a coppery luster. Depending on the seed supplier, orach comes in red, green, and buff-yellow. We often use orach as a filler material in fall arrangements.

Growing About 4 to 5 weeks before the last frost, sow the seeds in a soilless mix. Once they've germinated and the seedlings are large enough to handle, transplant them to cell flats. After all danger of frost has passed, transplant the seedlings to a sunny location in the garden. Unfortunately, deer relish the tasty leaves and can quickly strip a plant down to its stems.

Harvesting Harvest the stems just before the seedpods have fully developed.

Drying Place the stems in a glycerin solution for 3 to 4 days. Once the stems have absorbed the solution, bundle 3 or 4 together with a rubber band and hang them upside down to dry.

CALLISTEPHUS CHINENSIS
China Aster
Annual

>·◆›·○·‹◆·⊰

Color Pink, rose, red, yellow, blue, lavender, purple, white
Height 8 in. – 32 in.
Spacing 8 in. – 12 in.
Sowing Depth ⅛ in.
Germination Temp 65°F – 70°F
Germination Time 5 – 14 days

Asters are available in dwarf and tall varieties. Both come in a wide range of vibrant hues. We grow the tall, cut-flower varieties with double blooms, such as the Princess series.

Growing About 4 to 6 weeks before the last frost, sow the seeds in a soilless mix. Once they've germinated, transplant the seedlings to cell flats. After all danger of frost has passed, transplant the seedlings to an area with rich, loamy soil and full sun.

Harvesting Harvest asters just before the blooms fully open. Cut the stems as long as possible; they can always be shortened for a particular arrangement.

Drying For best results, dry asters in silica gel. Recut the stems near the flower head and place the blossoms face up in a container of silica gel. Cover them with additional silica gel. Air-dry or silica-dry the stems separately. When both are completely dry, glue the flower heads back onto their stems (see pp. 61-63).

CARTHAMUS TINCTORIUS
Safflower
Annual

>·◆›·○·‹◆·⊰

Color Orange, yellow orange, cream
Height 24 in. – 36 in.
Spacing 9 in. – 12 in.
Sowing Depth ¼ in.
Germination Temp 60°F – 70°F
Germination Time 10 – 14 days

Safflower blossoms are bright orange, yellow-orange, or cream. They complement the warm hues of fall and are perfect for fall arrangements. If the plants are harvested before they bloom, the green buds and spiny bracts are a splendid foliage substitute.

Growing About 2 to 3 weeks before the last frost, fill a cell flat with soilless mix and sow single seeds into the individual cells. Cover them lightly with additional medium. When all danger of frost has passed, transplant the seedlings to a garden location with full sun and well-drained soil.

Harvesting Harvest the short-stemmed flowers that appear first for use in wreaths. Once the majority of flowers on the plant are in full bloom, harvest the main stem. To use safflower as a foliage substitute, harvest the entire plant when the buds have fully developed, but before the orange flower tufts appear.

Drying Bundle several stems together with a rubber band and hang them upside down to dry.

CELOSIA ARGENTEA
Cockscomb or Plumed Celosia
Annual

⋙━◆━○━◆━⋘

Color Pink, rose, red, orange, yellow
Height 12 in. – 30 in.
Spacing 12 in. – 16 in.
Sowing Depth Lightly cover
Germination Temp 70°F – 75°F
Germination Time 7 – 14 days

Celosia flowers are striking in form and come in a wide range of vibrant colors. Cockscomb, the crested form (*Celosia argentea* var. *cristata*), has fuzzy, convoluted flower heads that add instant texture to arrangements. The plumed form (*Celosia argentea* var. *plumosa*) has feathery blooms. Grow tall, long-stemmed cultivars from series such as Chief (crested) and Century (plumed, shown above) for use in arrangements.

Growing About 4 to 6 weeks before the last frost, fill a flat with soilless mix and sow the seeds on the surface (barely cover the seeds with additional medium). Once they've germinated, transplant the seedlings to cell flats. After all danger of frost has passed, transplant them to a sunny area in the garden and keep the soil evenly moist.

Harvesting Cut the stems when the flowers are in full bloom. Strip the foliage off the lower portion of each stem.

Drying Bundle 3 or 4 stems together with a rubber band and hang them upside down to dry.

CELOSIA ARGENTEA VAR. SPICATA
Wheat Celosia
Annual

⋙━◆━○━◆━⋘

Color Pink, rosy-purple
Height 30 in. – 40 in.
Spacing 12 in.
Sowing Depth Lightly cover
Germination Temp 70°F – 75°F
Germination Time 7 – 14 days

The tall, multiple stems of wheat celosia are topped with pointed, feathery blooms. The cultivar 'Flamingo Feather' (shown above) has beautiful silvery-pink flowers, while 'Flamingo Purple' has rosy-purple blooms and attractive green-maroon stems and foliage. Both are easy to grow and wonderful additions to a dried flower garden and its future arrangements.

Growing About 4 weeks before the last frost, fill a flat with soilless mix and sow the seeds on the surface (barely cover the seeds with additional medium). Once they've germinated, transplant the seedlings to cell flats. After all danger of frost has passed, transplant them to a sunny area in the garden and keep the soil evenly moist.

Harvesting Harvest the stems when the majority of blooms have elongated but before they fully mature.

Drying Bundle several stems together with a rubber band and hang them upside down to dry. Handle these flowers carefully; they tend to shatter easily even if picked at their optimum time.

CENTAUREA MACROCEPHALA
Knapweed
Perennial

❯━◀▸━◦━◂◆━

Color Yellow
Height 36 in. – 48 in.
Spacing 18 in. – 24 in.
Sowing Depth ⅛ in.
Germination Temp 60°F – 70°F
Germination Time 5 – 10 days

Knapweed has puffy, bright yellow blooms that emerge from a base of scaly, brown bracts. These thistlelike flowers air-dry easily but darken to a muted shade of yellow. The color and coarse texture of knapweed blend well with rustic fall arrangements.

Growing About 6 to 8 weeks before the last frost, sow the seeds in a soilless mix. Once they've germinated and the seedlings are large enough to handle, transplant them to cell flats. After all danger of frost has past, transplant them to a sunny location in the garden. They do best in areas with warm days and cool nights.

Harvesting Cut the stems when the flowers are in full bloom. The substantial size of these flowers makes them perfect for large arrangements, so cut the stems long. Strip the foliage off the lower portion of each stem.

Drying Bundle 3 or 4 stems together with a rubber band and hang them upside down to dry in a warm, dark location. Knapweed can also be dried in silica gel.

CONSOLIDA
Larkspur
Annual

❯━◀▸━◦━◂◆━

Color Pink, blue, lavender, white
Height 24 in. – 48 in.
Spacing 9 in. – 12 in.
Sowing Depth ⅛ in.
Germination Temp 50°F – 55°F
Germination Time 20 – 25 days

Larkspur is one of our favorite dried flowers because it retains its vibrant hues when dry. We grow *Consolida ambigua*, Giant Imperial series, because it has closely spaced double florets. *Consolida orientalis* is similar and also dries well.

Growing Larkspur seeds can be sown directly in the garden, but we prefer to start them in flats. Prior to sowing, prechill the seed packets in the refrigerator for 7 to 14 days. About 4 to 6 weeks before the last frost, sow the seeds in a soilless mix and cover them with additional medium (darkness aids in germination). Keep the flat in a cool location. Once the seeds have germinated, transplant the seedlings to cell flats. When 4 true leaves fully develop, transplant them to a sunny location in the garden. The seedlings' growth will be stunted if they become root-bound in the cell flat.

Harvesting Harvest the flower spikes when the florets at the bottom of the stem have fully opened but before seedpods start to form in their centers. The petals will drop if the flowers are picked too late.

Drying Bundle 6 to 8 stems together with a rubber band and hang them upside down to dry.

CORNUS
Dogwood
Deciduous Tree or Shrub

>-!-<>-0-<>-!-<

Color Pink, cream
Height 7 ft. – 60 ft.
Spacing 15 ft. – 20 ft.
Planting Depth Same as container
Planting Time Spring or fall
Harvest Time Spring

In the landscape, dogwood trees offer flowers in spring, shady foliage in summer, and colorful leaves in fall. In arrangements, the delicate flowers offer a simple elegance. They are stunning when arranged together on a branch as they would be found in nature. *Cornus florida* is a popular landscape species and is excellent for drying.

Growing Purchase a dogwood tree from your local nursery and plant it in full sun or light shade. With regular watering, the tree will grow well in average garden soil.

Harvesting When fully developed, cut the flower heads from their branches. Harvest the branches in mid to late summer once the foliage has matured.

Drying Dry the flowers in silica gel. Once dry, they can be used individually on wreaths or reattached to branches for use in arrangements. Cut the leaves off the branches and dry them in silica gel. Air-dry the branches. See pp. 61-63 for details on reconstructing a branch.

CRASPEDIA GLOBOSA
Drumstick
Annual

>-!-<>-0-<>-!-<

Color Yellow
Height 24 in. – 30 in.
Spacing 9 in. – 12 in.
Sowing Depth ⅛ in.
Germination Temp 65°F – 70°F
Germination Time 10 – 20 days

The flower heads of *Craspedia* are composed of many tiny florets clustered together to form a perfect sphere. These 1-in. yellow balls sit atop strong, nearly leafless stems resembling a child's drumstick. Although small, these unusual flowers provide bright accents to summer and fall arrangements. *Craspedia* is a perennial in Zones 7 to 10; however, it is usually grown as an annual.

Growing Sow the seeds in late winter or early spring in a soilless mix. Once they've germinated, transplant the seedlings to individual cell flats and grow them in a cold frame until all danger of frost has passed. Transplant the seedlings to a sunny garden location with well-drained soil.

Harvesting Harvest *Craspedia* flowers when they are bright yellow and have fully opened. Cut the stems long; you can always shorten them for a particular arrangement.

Drying Bundle several stems together with a rubber band and hang them upside down to dry in a warm, dark location.

CYNARA CARDUNCULUS
Cardoon
Tender Perennial

>-↔-O-↔-<

Color Purple
Height 6 ft. – 8 ft. or more
Spacing 36 in.
Sowing Depth ⅛ in.
Germination Temp 60°F – 70°F
Germination Time 14 – 30 days

Closely related to globe artichokes, cardoons are usually grown as an annual vegetable. (Their blanched leaf stalks are used in soups and stews.) However, it's a perennial in Zones 6 to 9 and blooms in its second year from seed. In northern regions try growing it in tubs and protecting it during the winter. The thistlelike blooms are impressive in size and command attention in large arrangements.

Growing In late winter, sow the seeds in 4-in. pots. Keep them in a warm location (treat them as you would tomatoes). If the seeds grow quickly, transplant them to 1-gallon pots before they become root-bound. After all danger of frost has passed, transplant them to a sunny location in the garden.

Harvesting Harvest the blooms at various stages of growth. Cut some while in bud and others just as they begin to open and show a tuft of purple. The flowers will continue to open as they dry.

Drying Bundle 2 or 3 stems together and hang them in a warm, dark location. It may take 2 to 3 weeks for the thick stems and flower heads to dry.

DAHLIA
Dahlia
Tuberous-Rooted Perennial

>-↔-O-↔-<

Color Pink, rose, red, orange, yellow, purple, white
Height 8 in. – 48 in.
Spacing 12 in. – 36 in.
Planting Depth 6 in.
Planting Time Spring
Harvest Time Late summer to early fall

Choose dahlias for bright, continuous blooms from late summer until the first frost of fall. While some catalogs boast "flowers as large as dinner plates," it's best to grow either dwarf or tall varieties with small- to medium-size blooms for drying.

Growing In the spring, purchase dahlia tubers from your local garden center or preorder them from a catalog during the winter. Choose an area of the garden with full sun and well-drained soil. After all danger of frost has passed, cultivate the soil to a depth of 12 in. and amend it with peat moss or compost. Remove half the soil, place the tubers flat, and backfill. Tall varieties require staking.

Harvesting Harvest dahlias just before the blooms fully open, leaving 1 in. of stem attached to the flower head. Harvest a length of stem at the same time if you plan to reattach the dried dahlia flower later on.

Drying Cut the leaves off the stems. Dry the leaves, stems, and flower heads in silica gel. See pp. 61-63 for details on reconstructing entire flower stems, or glue the flower heads onto wires.

DELPHINIUM HYBRIDS
Delphinium
Perennial

>⊷⊶◦⊷⊶<

Color Pink, blue, lavender, purple, white
Height 24 in. – 72 in.
Spacing 12 in. – 18 in.
Sowing Depth 1/16 in.
Germination Temp 50°F – 55°F
Germination Time 14 – 28 days

It's easy to create dramatic flower arrangements using spires of delphinium. We grow Pacific Giant hybrids because they are mildew resistant and nearly 95% will have large double florets.

Growing Prior to sowing, prechill the seed packets in the refrigerator for about 2 weeks. Sow the seeds in late February and keep the seed flat in a cool location (a cool basement or insulated garage works well). High temperatures during the sowing process hinder germination. When large enough to handle, transplant the seedlings to cell flats. After all danger of frost has passed, transplant the seedlings to a sunny location in a well-amended garden and stake the tall stems as they grow. Delphinium plants are heavy feeders and will require an application of an all-purpose fertilizer in subsequent years. No additional fertilizer is needed the year they are planted.

Harvesting Harvest the flower spikes before the bottom florets shed their petals. If picked too late, the majority of petals will drop as they dry. After harvesting the first set of flowers, cut the plant back for a second blooming later in the season.

Drying Hang the flower spikes upside down either individually or in small bundles of 3 or 4 stems.

ECHINACEA PURPUREA
Purple Coneflower
Perennial

>⊷⊶◦⊷⊶<

Color Seed head: Orange-brown
Height 30 in. – 48 in.
Spacing 12 in. – 16 in.
Sowing Depth 1/8 in.
Germination Temp 65°F – 70°F
Germination Time 10 – 21 days

The name *Echinacea* is derived from the Greek word *echinos*, for hedgehog. It refers to the flower's prickly, cone-shaped center. Enjoy the daisylike blooms in your garden throughout the summer. At summer's end, remove the petals and dry the orange-brown seed heads for use in fall arrangements.

Growing In mid-March, sow the seeds in a soilless mix and lightly cover them with additional medium. Once they've germinated and the seedlings are large enough to handle, transplant them to cell flats. After all danger of frost has passed, transplant them to a garden location with full sun and well-drained soil. *Echinacea* often flowers its first year from seed.

Harvesting Cut the stems when the center cone is fully developed, and strip off the petals and foliage.

Drying Bundle 4 to 6 stems together with a rubber band and hang them upside down to dry in a warm, dark location.

ECHINOPS
Globe Thistle
Perennial

➤┤◆➤━O━◆├◀┤◀

Color Steel-blue
Height 36 in. – 60 in.
Spacing 18 in. – 24 in.
Sowing Depth ⅛ in.
Germination Temp 65°F – 70°F
Germination Time 14 – 21 days

As its common name implies, globe thistle adds wonderful form and texture to dried floral projects. This steel-blue flower blends well with other cool colors in winter arrangements. *Echinops bannaticus* grows to 5 ft., while *Echinops ritro* stands at about 3½ ft. They have similar flowers and both are excellent for drying.

Growing About 6 to 8 weeks before the last frost, sow the seeds in a soilless mix and cover them with additional medium. Once they've germinated, transplant the seedlings to cell flats and grow them in a cold frame. After all danger of frost has passed, transplant them to a sunny location in the garden where their roots will receive even moisture.

Harvesting Wear gloves to harvest these prickly flowers. Cut the stems when the bracts are steel-blue but before they open into florets. If picked too late, the bristly spheres may shatter when dry.

Drying Bundle several stems together with a rubber band and hang them upside down to dry in a warm, dark location.

ERYNGIUM
Sea Holly
Perennial/Biennial

➤┤◆➤━O━◆├◀┤◀

Color Gray-green, steel-blue
Height 24 in. – 48 in.
Spacing 18 in. – 24 in.
Sowing Depth Surface-sow
Germination Temp 60°F – 65°F
Germination Time 2 – 3 weeks or longer (irregular)

The spiny blooms of *Eryngium* provide interesting color and texture to fall and winter arrangements. The large thistly blooms of *Eryngium giganteum* (shown above) are a beautiful gray-green when they mature. *Eryngium alpinum* and *Eryngium planum* are both a striking steel-blue color, but each has its own unique flower.

Growing Fresh *Eryngium* seeds have the best chance of germinating. In the fall, fill a flat with soilless mix and lightly press the seeds into contact with the medium. Cold temperatures are necessary to break the seeds' dormancy, so place the flat in a cold frame to overwinter. Once the seeds have germinated in the spring, transplant the seedlings to the garden in an area of well-drained soil and full sun. Avoid overwatering.

Harvesting Harvest the fully developed flower heads when they turn steel-blue or gray-green (depending on the variety). Wire the individual blooms (see p. 61) or harvest entire branches when the majority of flower heads are in their prime.

Drying Dry wired flower heads standing upright in jars. Dry branches by bundling 2 or 3 together with a rubber band then hanging them upside down.

EUCALYPTUS CINEREA
Gum Tree
Evergreen Tree or Shrub

GOMPHRENA
Globe Amaranth
Annual

Color Green
Height 3 ft. – 90 ft.
Spacing 12 in. (grown as annual)
Sowing Depth Surface-sow
Germination Temp 70°F – 75°F
Germination Time 7 – 21 days

Color Pink, rose, red, carmine, orange, purple, white
Height 18 in. – 24 in.
Spacing 10 in. – 12 in.
Sowing Depth ⅛ in.
Germination Temp 70°F – 75°F
Germination Time 5 – 20 days

Most *Eucalyptus* trees are hardy only in Zones 9 to 10. However, we grow them as annuals. In a single season, *Eucalyptus cinerea* 'Silver Dollar' (shown above) and 'Silver Plate' grow 2 ft. to 3 ft. tall. Both are commonly grown for flower-arranging material.

Growing About 10 weeks before the last frost, fill a flat with soilless mix and sow the seeds on the surface. Once they've germinated, transplant the seedlings to cell flats. After all danger of frost has passed, transplant them to a sunny location in the garden. In cold regions, grow *Eucalyptus* as an annual by mulching with black plastic and spacing the plants 12 in. apart. In warm regions, grow it as a tree or shrub and space accordingly.

Harvesting Once the leaves mature at summer's end, cut the single stems at their bases. In our area (Zone 7), we harvest the single stems and heavily mulch the stumps and roots. They usually come back the following year as multibranched shrubs.

Drying Preserve *Eucalyptus* with glycerin, and hang small bundles of the stems upside down to dry. Alternately, dry *Eucalyptus* in silica gel.

Globe amaranth is one of the easiest dried flowers to grow—it readily starts from seed, it tolerates heat and drought, it grows in a wide range of soil types, it blooms all summer, and it provides dried flowers that retain their natural form and vibrant hues. *Gomphrena globosa* comes in a variety of colors including white, rose, pink, and purple. *Gomphrena haageana* offers red, orange, and carmine blooms (shown above).

Growing About 6 weeks before the last frost, sow the seeds in a soilless mix. Once they've germinated and the seedlings are large enough to handle, transplant them to cell flats. After all danger of frost has passed, transplant them to a sunny location in the garden.

Harvesting Globe amaranth is ready to harvest when the flower heads are about ¾ in. long and their stems are stiff. If picked too early, the dried, immature stems may not be strong enough to hold up the flower heads in humid conditions.

Drying Bundle several stems together with a rubber band and hang them upside down to dry in a dark location.

GYPSOPHILA PANICULATA
Baby's Breath
Perennial

>—+◆>—○—<◆+—<

Color White
Height 36 in.
Spacing 18 in. – 24 in.
Sowing Depth Lightly cover
Germination Temp 70°F – 75°F
Germination Time 10 – 15 days

Baby's breath is a popular filler flower that lends a light and airy feel to fresh and dried arrangements. The flowers shrink during the drying process, so it's important to grow the large, double-flowered varieties. The cultivar 'Double Snowflake' (shown above) is easily propagated from seed and approximately 50% of the plants produce double flowers.

Growing About 6 to 8 weeks before the last frost, sow the seeds in a soilless mix and cover them lightly with additional medium. Once they've germinated, transplant the seedlings to cell flats. After all danger of frost has passed transplant them to a garden location with full sun and well-drained soil.

Harvesting Cut the stems when the flowers are in full bloom. Once the flowers are past their prime, the creamy white petals turn brown and are unattractive in arrangements.

Drying Bundle several stems together with a rubber band and hang them upside down to dry in a dark location.

HELIANTHUS ANNUUS
Sunflowers
Annual

>—+◆>—○—<◆+—<

Color Red-orange, yellow, cream
Height 12 in. – 120 in.
Spacing 18 in. – 24 in.
Sowing Depth ¼ in.
Germination Temp 70°F – 75°F
Germination Time 5 – 10 days

Make your summer and fall arrangements come alive with sunflowers. For easy drying, choose cultivars that produce multiple side branches with smaller flowers, such as 'Sonja', 'Pacino' (shown above), 'Sundance Kid', and 'Holiday'.

Growing Sow sunflower seeds directly in the garden after all danger of frost has passed. Alternately, start them indoors in 3-in. to 4-in. pots 2 to 3 weeks before the last frost. The seedlings should not grow in these pots longer than 4 weeks before they are transplanted to the garden. Locate the plants in full sun and well-drained soil.

Harvesting Harvest the flowers in full bloom, leaving the stem length as long as possible.

Drying These dramatic flowers look best when they are dried in silica gel. Trim the stem to fit the length of your silica gel container. Place the flower head face up and cover it with additional silica gel. The petals will dry in 2 to 3 days, but leave the flower in the container for several extra days to ensure the thick stem has time to dry.

HELICHRYSUM BRACTEATUM
Strawflower
Annual

⊱―◆―○―◆―⊰

Color Pink, rose, red, orange, peach, apricot, yellow, white
Height 12 in. – 48 in.
Spacing 10 in. – 12 in.
Sowing Depth Surface-sow
Germination Temp 70°F – 75°F
Germination Time 7 – 10 days

Comprised of stiff, papery bracts, strawflower blossoms feel dry even when they're fresh. We grow *Helichrysum bracteatum* var. *monstrosum* for its large double blooms.

Growing About 4 to 6 weeks before the last frost, fill a flat with soilless mix and sow the seeds on the surface. Once they've germinated and the seedlings are large enough to handle, transplant them to cell flats. After all danger of frost has past, transplant them to a garden location with full sun and well-drained soil.

Harvesting Harvest the flowers when the first row or two of bracts open. They will continue to open as they dry. A flower that is picked too late will open completely and expose an unattractive center. Harvest and wire the flower heads (see p. 61) or harvest the stems with the flowers attached.

Drying Place the wired flower heads upright in jars to dry. If the stems are attached, bundle and hang them to dry. However, the dried stems may not be strong enough to hold up the flower heads in humid conditions.

HELICHRYSUM CASSIANUM
Rose Beauty
Annual

⊱―◆―○―◆―⊰

Color Pink
Height 18 in. – 24 in.
Spacing 10 in. – 12 in.
Sowing Depth Surface-sow
Germination Temp 70°F – 75°F
Germination Time 5 – 14 days

The papery pink flowers of rose beauty are well suited for small arrangements. Unfortunately, their stems shrivel during the drying process and are too weak to hold up the flower heads in humid conditions. As a solution, attach small clusters of the diminutive flowers to a wire or pick (see p. 61). Once supported, these delicate blooms beautifully enhance spring and summer arrangements.

Growing About 4 to 5 weeks before the last frost, fill a flat with soilless mix and sow the seeds on the surface. Once they've germinated, transplant the seedlings to cell flats. After all danger of frost has passed, transplant them to a sunny location in the garden.

Harvesting Harvest the stems as the majority of flowers in the cluster come into full bloom; some florets will remain in bud. If the flowers are picked too late, the small yellow centers release a puff of dandelion-like seeds during the drying process.

Drying Bundle several stems together with a rubber band and hang them upside down to dry.

HELLEBORUS
Hellebore
Perennial

⊱⊶⊷⊷◦⊶⊷⊶⊰

Color Pink, maroon, yellow-green, green, white
Height 12 in. – 24 in.
Spacing 12 in. – 16 in.
Sowing Depth 1/16 in.
Germination Temp See below
Germination Time 140 – 280 days

Hellebores bloom during the winter and add as much charm to a winter garden as they do to a dried arrangement. *Helleborus foetidus* (shown above) has wonderful green, bell-shaped flowers that can be used as a foliage substitute. *Helleborus orientalis* also dries well and comes in a range of lovely, muted hues.

Growing The easiest way to obtain hellebores is to buy a nursery-grown plant and let it self-seed. If you decide to grow them yourself, use fresh seeds to increase the odds of germination. Sow the seeds in a soilless mix. To break their dormancy, they will require 6 weeks at 70°F or higher. Then lower the temperature to 25°F to 32°F for 6 to 8 weeks. Slowly increase the temperature; the seeds should germinate as the soil warms. If they do not germinate in 4 to 6 weeks, repeat the process using the same flat of seeds.

Harvesting Cut the stems when the flowers are in full bloom.

Drying Dry the flower sprays (including their stems) on their sides in silica gel.

HUMULUS LUPULUS
Hop
Perennial Vine

⊱⊶⊷⊷◦⊶⊷⊶⊰

Color Green
Height 15 ft. – 25 ft.
Spacing 36 in.
Planting Depth 1 in. – 2 in.
Planting Time Spring
Harvest Time Late summer or early fall

Comprised of clustered bracts, hop flowers look like delicate green cones and are a key ingredient in beer production. Female plants bare these flowers, but no male pollinator is necessary. This vigorous climber requires a sturdy arbor or trellis for support. Its far-reaching vines grow during the spring and summer but die back to the ground in winter. Although hop flowers develop in late summer and early fall, their fresh, apple-green color makes them perfect for dried spring arrangements.

Growing While hops can be grown from seed, it's best to buy root cuttings from a plant catalog or your local nursery. Typically these suppliers sell cuttings from female rootstock to ensure production of the conelike flowers. Plant cuttings in rich, fertile soil, just below the surface.

Harvesting Harvest the vines in late summer or early fall when the flowers are fully developed. Cut the long vines for use in garlands, or harvest the short lateral stems for use in arrangements.

Drying Bundle 3 or 4 stems together with a rubber band and hang them upside down to dry. Hang the long vines individually.

HYACINTHUS
Hyacinth
Bulb

⊱┄◈┄◦┄◈┄⊰

Color Pink, rose, peach, light yellow, blue, lavender, purple, white
Height 8 in. – 12 in.
Spacing 6 in.
Planting Depth 4 in. – 6 in.
Planting Time Fall
Harvest Time Spring

The heady fragrance of hyacinths makes them a welcome addition to spring gardens. If you prefer, grow them indoors in a hyacinth glass and fill your home with their lovely scent. The large, colorful flower spikes are delightful focal-point flowers in spring arrangements.

Growing In the fall, purchase hyacinth bulbs from your local garden center or order them from a catalog during the summer. Choose an area of the garden with full sun and well-drained soil. Amend the soil with peat moss or compost, sand, and bone meal or bulb fertilizer. Plant the bulbs in late fall; they will bloom the following spring.

Harvesting Harvest the flowers when they are in full bloom. Cut the stems near their bases.

Drying Once the flowers are cut, insert a wire into the stem and dry the blooms on their sides in silica gel (see pp. 40-43 for details). When the flowers are dry, spray them with a surface sealer. Because their color tends to fade, also apply colored floral sprays.

HYDRANGEA
Hydrangea
Deciduous Shrub

⊱┄◈┄◦┄◈┄⊰

Color Pink, blue, lavender, cream
Height 5 ft. – 20 ft.
Spacing 6 ft. – 10 ft.
Planting Depth Same as container
Planting Time Spring or fall
Harvest Time Summer and fall

Hydrangeas dry easily and offer splendid blooms for large arrangements. We dry two species. The mophead form of bigleaf hydrangeas (*Hydrangea macrophylla*) produces large, clustered flower heads (shown above). They are hardy in Zones 6 or 7 to 9 but can be grown in 15-gallon containers in colder regions with winter protection. Peegee hydrangea (*Hydrangea paniculata 'Grandiflora'*) is hardier (to Zone 5) and has large conical clusters of cream-colored florets that turn salmon-pink in the fall.

Growing Purchase hydrangea plants from a catalog or your local nursery. Plant them in rich, moist soil that receives sun or partial shade (a semishady location is important in hot climates).

Harvesting To air-dry hydrangeas, harvest them in late summer or early fall after the flowers change color and become leathery. To preserve their bright summer colors, harvest the blossoms before they change and dry them in silica gel.

Drying Depending on when you harvest, either bundle several stems together with a rubber band and hang them upside down to dry, or place the flowers face up in a container of silica gel and cover them with additional silica gel.

IRIS FOETIDISSIMA
Scarlet-Seeded Iris, Gladwin Iris
Perennial

>─┼─◇─┼◇┼─◇─┼─<

Color Seeds: red-orange
Height 18 in. – 24 in.
Spacing 12 in. – 18 in.
Sowing Depth ⅛ in.
Germination Temp See below
Germination Time At least 30 days

Although the small flowers of *Iris foetidissima* are not showy, the seeds are a vibrant orange. In the fall, the green seedpods split open to reveal the colorful seeds. They remain attached to the pod throughout the fall. The glossy, evergreen foliage will add interest to your winter garden while the bright seedpods will enhance your fall arrangements.

Growing Use a utility knife to nick the outer coat of each seed. About 10 to 12 weeks before the last frost, sow the seeds in a soilless mix and keep the flat at 65°F to 70°F for 2 to 4 weeks. Then move the flat to the refrigerator for 4 to 6 weeks. Remove the flat and keep it between 40°F to 55°F until the seeds germinate. After all danger of frost has passed, transplant them to the garden in an area of partial or full shade. This accommodating plant tolerates dry soil and will form large clumps.

Harvesting Cut the stems soon after the seedpods split open.

Drying Bundle several stems together with a rubber band and hang them upside down to dry. The seeds shrivel and turn red-orange when they're completely dry.

LIATRIS SPICATA
Blazing Star, Gayfeather
Perennial

>─┼─◇─┼◇┼─◇─┼─<

Color Violet, white
Height 18 in. – 36 in.
Spacing 4 in. – 6 in.
Sowing Depth Surface-sow
Germination Temp 70°F – 75°F
Germination Time 14 – 21 days

With its delightful fuzzy texture and striking violet hue, *Liatris* is a wonderful addition to dried arrangements. The cultivar 'Kobold' stands about 18 in. tall, while 'Floristan Violet' and 'Floristan White' grow to a stately 3 ft.

Growing Purchase *Liatris* corms from your local garden center in early spring, or grow them yourself from seed. About 6 to 8 weeks before the last frost, sow the seeds in a soilless mix by pressing them into the medium without covering them. Once they've germinated, transplant the seedlings to cell flats. After all danger of frost has passed, transplant the seedlings to a garden location with full sun and well-drained soil. *Liatris* may develop a single flower spike in its first year from seed.

Harvesting The flower spikes bloom from the top down. Allow the majority of buds to fully open, but harvest the spike before the top florets begin to wither.

Drying Strip the grasslike leaves off the bottom of the stems, and bundle 3 or 4 flower spikes together with a rubber band. Hang them upside down to dry.

LIGUSTRUM JAPONICUM
Wax-Leaf Privet
Evergreen Shrub

>—I—●>—O—<●—I—<

Color White
Height 10 ft. – 12 ft.
Spacing 48 in. – 72 in.
Planting Depth Same as container
Planting Time Spring through fall
Harvest Time Spring and summer

This evergreen shrub is used for hedges and topiaries in Zones 7 to 10. In colder regions, wax-leaf privet can be grown in tubs if shelter is provided during the winter. We use both the flowers and leaves in our dried arrangements. Unfortunately, shearing the plants into hedges or topiaries removes the flowering branches. For arranging material, allow one plant to grow naturally and harvest the flowers and branches judiciously.

Growing Purchase wax-leaf privet plants from your local nursery. They grow easily in average garden soil. Choose a location with full sun or partial shade.

Harvesting Harvest the flowers in full bud or just before full bloom. Harvest the branches in mid to late summer once the leaves have matured and stiffened.

Drying Lay the blooms on their sides in a container of silica gel and cover them with additional silica gel. Once dry, they are very fragile and must be handled and arranged with care. Spray them with polyurethane for added strength. Dry the leaves and branches in silica gel.

LILIUM
Lily
Bulb

>—I—●>—O—<●—I—<

Color Pink, red, orange, apricot, yellow, white
Height 20 in. – 40 in.
Spacing 6 in.
Planting Depth 6 in. – 8 in.
Planting Time Fall or spring
Harvest Time Summer

Lilies add a graceful air to landscapes and arrangements. We grow and dry Asiatic lilies (shown above), but other varieties such as oriental and trumpet lilies are also worthy of experimentation. Use individual blossoms on wreaths, or reconstruct entire stems for focal points in large arrangements.

Growing Lily bulbs can be purchased in either the fall or the spring; plant them as soon as you acquire them. Choose an area in full sun with surrounding foliage to shade their roots. Amend the soil with peat moss or compost and sand. Fertilize in the spring and on a monthly basis until the blossoms fade.

Harvesting Cut the flowers when they are in full bloom. If you plan to reconstruct an entire stem, harvest the buds as well. In mid to late summer, harvest the top 12 in. of stem once the foliage has matured.

Drying Dry the individual blossoms and buds in silica gel. Later in the summer, dry the stems in silica gel. Once all the flower parts are dry, apply a surface sealer and colored floral sprays. See pp. 61-63 for details on reconstructing entire flower stems.

LIMONIUM LATIFOLIUM
Sea Lavender
Perennial

>━┅◆┅○┅◆┅━<

Color Lavender
Height 18 in. – 24 in.
Spacing 16 in. – 20 in.
Sowing Depth ⅛ in.
Germination Temp 65°F – 70°F
Germination Time 10 – 20 days

Growing from a basal clump of leathery leaves, sea lavender produces sprays of airy stems covered in dainty lavender blooms.
The flowers are composed of a white, papery calyx with an inner
bluish-lavender corolla. This filler flower is a good substitute
for baby's breath. Sea lavender is perfect for arrangements needing
a hint of color to complement larger focal-point flowers. It is
easy to grow, drought-resistant, and blooms in its second year
from seed.

Growing About 4 to 6 weeks before the last frost, sow the seeds
in a soilless mix. Once they've germinated and the seedlings are
large enough to handle, transplant them to cell flats. After all danger of frost has passed, transplant them to a garden location with
full sun and well-drained soil.

Harvesting Harvest the stems when the majority of flowers are in
full bloom.

Drying Bundle 3 or 4 stems together with a rubber band and
hang them upside down to dry.

LIMONIUM SINUATUM
Statice
Annual

>━┅◆┅○┅◆┅━<

Color Rose, apricot, yellow, blue, purple, white
Height 18 in. – 24 in.
Spacing 12 in.
Sowing Depth ⅛ in.
Germination Temp 65°F – 70°F
Germination Time 5 – 14 days

Statice is a staple everlasting in the dried-flower industry. It's easy
to grow and a prolific bloomer. The papery blooms dry quickly
and retain their form and vibrant colors. Statice is rarely used as a
focal point in arrangements, but it is indispensable as an accent
flower. We grow the Pacific series for its long stems and full
flower heads.

Growing About 4 to 6 weeks before the last frost, sow the seeds
in a soilless mix. Once they've germinated and the seedlings are
large enough to handle, transplant them to cell flats. After all
danger of frost has passed, transplant them to a garden location
with full sun and well-drained soil.

Harvesting Harvest the stems when the flowers are in full bloom.
Cut the stems close to the basal foliage; they can always be shortened for a particular arrangement.

Drying Bundle several stems together with a rubber band and
hang them upside down to dry. Keep the bundles moderately sized
or mold may develop on the stems.

LIMONIUM SUWOROWII
(PSYLLIOSTACHYS SUWOROWII)
Russian Statice
Annual

⊱━◆━○━◆━⊰

Color Rose
Height 18 in. – 24 in.
Spacing 10 in. – 12 in.
Sowing Depth 1/16 in.
Germination Temp 70°F – 75°F
Germination Time 5 – 14 days

The leafless stems of Russian statice are covered with minute, rosy florets. The first flower spikes to bloom in midsummer are the tallest. The plants will continue to produce shorter stems until frost.

Growing About 2 to 3 weeks before the last frost, sow the seeds in a soilless mix. Once they've germinated and the seedlings are large enough to handle, transplant them to cell flats. After danger of frost has passed, transplant them to a location with full sun and well-drained soil. Russian statice dislikes extremely hot, dry summer conditions. For best results, keep the soil evenly moist and protect the plants with a lath or shade cover on excessively hot, sunny days.

Harvesting Cut the stems when the flower spikes are almost in full bloom.

Drying Bundle several stems together with a rubber band and hang them upside down to dry. Although the stems will remain stiff after drying, it's advisable to spray the flower spikes with a sealer (the tips have a tendency to droop in humid conditions).

LIMONIUM TATARICUM
(GONIOLIMON TATARICUM)
German Statice
Perennial

⊱━◆━○━◆━⊰

Color White
Height 18 in. – 20 in.
Spacing 12 in. – 18 in.
Sowing Depth 1/8 in.
Germination Temp 65°F – 70°F
Germination Time 10 – 20 days

German statice is a popular filler flower for everlasting arrangements. Hundreds of small starlike flowers form a canopy above stiff, multibranched stems. The papery blooms dry quickly and retain their form and bright white color. Once dry, the main stem can be cut into smaller pieces to accommodate any size arrangement. German statice produces a basal clump of leathery foliage the first year from seed and will bloom in the second year.

Growing About 4 to 6 weeks before the last frost, sow the seeds in a soilless mix. Once they've germinated, transplant the seedlings to cell flats. After all danger of frost has past, transplant them to a garden location with full sun and well-drained soil. German statice tolerates summer heat, cold winters, and some drought.

Harvesting Harvest the stems when the majority of flowers are in full bloom.

Drying Bundle 3 or 4 stems together with a rubber band and hang them upside down to dry.

LUNARIA ANNUA
Money Plant, Honesty, Silver Dollar
Biennial

>─┤◆>─○─<◆┤─<

Color Pods: green, silvery-white
Height 24 in. – 36 in.
Spacing 12 in. – 18 in.
Sowing Depth ⅛ in.
Germination Temp 65°F – 70°F
Germination Time 10 – 14 days

Lunaria is grown for its seedpods. If harvested early, the flat, green pods are a wonderful foliage substitute in arrangements. If left to mature, the seedpods turn brown and open to reveal a silvery-white center membrane.

Growing In late spring, fill a cell flat with soilless mix and place one seed in each cell. The seedlings will grow in the flat without further transplanting until it's time to plant them in the garden. After all danger of frost has passed, plant the seedlings in a sunny location (or partial shade in hot climates). The plants will flower and produce pods the following year.

Harvesting To use the seedpods as a foliage substitute, harvest the stems when the pods have fully developed yet still retain their green color. Alternately, to reveal the silvery membrane inside, harvest the pods when they have turned brown. Once they are dry, gently peel off the two outer sides of the pod.

Drying Dry the stems standing upright in buckets or hang them upside down in small bundles. Use colored floral sprays to maintain the plant's original green color.

MOLUCCELLA LAEVIS
Bells of Ireland
Annual

>─┤◆>─○─<◆┤─<

Color Green
Height 24 in. – 42 in.
Spacing 12 in. – 16 in.
Sowing Depth Lightly cover
Germination Temp See below
Germination Time 14 – 30 days (irregular)

Green bell-shaped calyces ring the long stems of bells of Ireland, each with a tiny white flower in the center.

Growing About 8 to 10 weeks before the last frost, fill a seed tray with soilless mix. Sow the seeds on the surface and barely cover them with additional medium. Place the tray in the refrigerator for 1 to 2 weeks (keep moist). Then remove the tray and provide 60°F to 70°F daytime temperatures and 55°F night temperatures. The seeds will germinate sporadically over several weeks. Transplant them to cell flats. After all danger of frost has passed, transplant them to a sunny garden.

Harvesting Harvest the stems when the majority of calyces are mature and stiff but still green. Trim off the top 2 in. to 3 in. of immature stem and remove the foliage.

Drying Bundle 3 or 4 stems together and hang them upside down to dry. Alternately, preserve the stems in glycerin before drying to reduce shattering. Once dry, the stem and calyces quickly fade to light beige. This natural color works well in fall arrangements, or you can restore their original green color with colored floral sprays.

NARCISSUS
Daffodil
Bulb

⊷⊶⊙⊶⊷

Color Yellow, cream
Height 6 in. – 18 in.
Spacing 6 in.
Planting Depth 6 in. – 8 in.
Planting Time Fall
Harvest Time Spring

Daffodils are the true harbingers of spring. Their bright colors enliven their surroundings, whether it's a leafless landscape or a spring arrangement. For drying, choose cultivars with thick petals such as the classic 'King Alfred'.

Growing In the fall, purchase daffodil bulbs from your local garden center or order them from a catalog during the summer. Choose an area of the garden with full sun and well-drained soil. Amend the soil with peat moss or compost, sand, and bone meal or bulb fertilizer. Plant the bulbs in late fall; they will bloom the following spring.

Harvesting Harvest the blooms when fully open. Cut the stems 8 in. to 10 in. long and temporarily place them in a vase of water while you complete the following step.

Drying Once the flowers are cut, insert a wire into the stem and dry the blooms in silica gel (see pp. 40-43 for details). When the flowers are dry, spray them with several light coats of a surface sealer. The blooms hold their bright yellow color even after drying.

NIGELLA
Love-in-a-Mist
Annual

⊷⊶⊙⊶⊷

Color Pods: green, maroon; flowers: pink, rose, blue, white
Height 18 in. – 24 in.
Spacing 9 in. – 12 in.
Sowing Depth 1/16 in.
Germination Temp 65°F – 70°F
Germination Time 10 – 15 days

Nigella is typically grown for its interesting seedpods, but the delicate flowers can also be dried. Cultivars of *Nigella damascena*, including 'Miss Jekyll', 'Persian Jewels', and 'Mulbury Rose', come in a range of colors. Other species include *Nigella orientalis* 'Transformer' and *Nigella hispanica* 'Exotica', each with uniquely shaped seedpods.

Growing Although *Nigella* seedlings dislike their roots being disturbed, we have not encountered any problems with sowing them in flats. About 4 to 6 weeks before the last frost, sow the seeds in a soilless mix. Immediately after they germinate, transplant the seedlings to cell flats. After all danger of frost has passed, transplant them to a sunny position in the garden. The seedlings' growth will be stunted if they become root-bound in the cell flat.

Harvesting Harvest the flowers when they are in full bloom. Harvest the pods when they have fully developed and their maroon stripes darken. Cut the entire plant at its base when the majority of pods are in their prime, or harvest the stems individually as the pods mature.

Drying Dry the flowers in silica gel. Dry the pods by hanging the entire plant or bundles of the individual stems upside down.

ORIGANUM VULGARE
Oregano
Perennial

➤┼◆➤─○─◄┼◄

Color Sage-green, purple
Height 18 in. – 24 in.
Spacing 12 in. – 16 in.
Sowing Depth Lightly cover
Germination Temp 60°F – 65°F
Germination Time 7 – 14 days

Grow oregano as a savory culinary herb, or use it as an equally pleasing filler flower in arrangements. While the leaves are used for cooking, it's the deep purple and sage-green bracts (not the whitish-lavender flowers) that are dried for arrangements. Oregano's deep hues are an important ingredient in fall and winter displays.

Growing Approximately 6 weeks before the last frost, sow the seeds in a soilless mix. Once they've germinated and the seedlings are large enough to handle, transplant them to cell flats. After all danger of frost has passed, transplant them to a garden location with full sun and well-drained soil.

Harvesting As the tiny whitish-lavender flowers fade, the remaining bracts will mature and stiffen. Harvest the stems when the majority of flowers have fallen but before the bracts discolor with age.

Drying Bundle several stems together with a rubber band and hang them upside down to dry.

ORNAMENTAL GRASSES
Annuals and Perennials

➤┼◆➤─○─◄┼◄

Color Maroon, green, beige
Height 18 in. – 72 in.
Spacing 12 in. – 36 in.
Sowing Depth Varies
Germination Temp 65°F – 70°F
Germination Time 7 – 28 days

Ornamental grasses offer interesting textures and muted hues. A few of our favorites include red switch grass (*Panicum violaceum*), foxtail millet (*Setaria italica*), feathertop (*Pennisetum villosum*), broomcorn (*Sorghum bicolor*), and grain crops such as wheat, oats, and barley.

Growing It's best to start ornamental grasses in cell flats rather than in the garden so that the tiny seedlings are not inadvertently pulled along with the common weed grasses. About 4 weeks before the last frost, evenly sprinkle the seeds over a cell flat filled with soilless mix (3 to 4 seeds in each cell). Cover the seeds with additional medium if the seed packet advises. No thinning is necessary. Simply transplant the cell plugs to a sunny location in the garden after all danger of frost has passed.

Harvesting Harvest the seed heads when fully developed but before the seeds are ripe. If picked too late, the seed heads may shatter.

Drying Bundle a handful of stems together with a rubber band and hang them upside down to dry. For graceful arches in the stems, experiment with drying them upright in buckets.

PAEONIA
Peony
Perennial

>—+◆>—○—<◆+—<

Color Pink, rose, red, white
Height 18 in. – 42 in.
Spacing 24 in. – 36 in.
Planting Depth 1 in. – 2 in.
Planting Time Spring or fall
Harvest Time Late spring and summer

Create dramatic focal points in your arrangements by incorporating large, perfectly preserved peony blossoms. These long-lived plants provide both flowers and foliage. Use the individual flower heads in wreaths and garlands, or reattach them to their dried stems for use in large arrangements.

Growing Purchase peony plants from a catalog or your local nursery. Choose a sunny location, and deeply amend the soil with thoroughly rotted manure or compost. Plant the roots so the eyes sit 1 in. to 2 in. below the soil surface. The large blossoms may require staking.

Harvesting In late spring, harvest peony flowers when they are in full bloom, leaving about 1 in. of stem attached to the head. If picked too late, the blossoms may shatter. Later in the summer, harvest the stems once the foliage has matured and stiffened.

Drying Air-dried peonies shrivel considerably, so dry them in silica gel. Place the flower heads face up and cover them with additional silica gel (make sure it reaches the center of each bloom). Air-dry the stems after removing the leaves. Dry the leaves in silica gel. See pp. 61-63 for details on how to reconstruct an entire stem.

PAPAVER SOMNIFERUM
Poppy
Annual

>—+◆>—○—<◆+—<

Color Pods: buff-gray
Height 24 in. – 48 in.
Spacing 12 in. – 14 in.
Sowing Depth Surface-sow
Germination Temp 60°F – 70°F
Germination Time 10 – 14 days

Delicate poppy flowers are short lived, but their woody seedpods last indefinitely in dried arrangements. The green, spherical pods turn a beautiful buff-gray as they mature. Use these natural-colored pods along with other seed heads and fall flowers in fall arrangements. Although there are many species within the genus, *Papaver somniferum* is most commonly used for arranging.

Growing Annual poppies germinate easily and are prolific self-seeders. Simply scatter the seeds in a sunny garden in early spring; once the seedlings are up, thin them to stand approximately 12 in. apart. We grow poppy seedlings in flats but transplant them to the garden long before they become root-bound. In windy areas, poppies may need staking.

Harvesting Harvest the pods once they mature and turn buff-gray. If picked too early, the pods will shrivel.

Drying Dry the pods upright in buckets or hang bundles upside down. If you hang-dry them, be aware that thousands of minute seeds will be released.

PHYSALIS ALKEKENGI
(PHYSALIS FRANCHETII)
Chinese Lantern
Perennial

>―+❖―o―❖+―<

Color Pods: orange
Height 18 in. – 24 in.
Spacing 10 in. – 12 in.
Sowing Depth Surface-sow
Germination Temp 70°F
Germination Time 7 – 30 days

Chinese lanterns are wonderful in fall arrangements and the perfect complement to fall displays containing pumpkins. The vibrant orange, lantern-shaped calyx that surrounds the fruit is papery and dries easily. Seeds for *Physalis alkekengi* are widely available, but for the largest lanterns, seek out the cultivar 'Gigantea'.

Growing In late winter, prior to sowing, prechill the seed packet in the refrigerator for 4 weeks. About 4 to 6 weeks before the last frost, fill a flat with soilless mix and sow the seeds on the surface. Once they've germinated, transplant the seedlings to cell flats. After all danger of frost has passed, transplant them to a sunny garden location and keep the soil evenly moist. Their underground runners will spread but are easy to pull.

Harvesting Cut the stems when the lanterns turn bright orange and remove the foliage.

Drying Stand the stems upright in buckets to dry, or place them on their sides in a cardboard box or on a drying rack.

ROSA
Rose
Deciduous Shrub

>―+❖―o―❖+―<

Color Pink, rose, red, orange, peach, yellow, lavender, white
Height 1 ft. – 20 ft.
Spacing 36 in. – 48 in.
Planting Depth Same as container
Planting Time Fall or spring
Harvest Time Late spring through summer

Rose petals are velvety yet somewhat thick, which makes them perfect candidates for drying. These time-honored flowers come in a wide range of colors, shapes, and sizes, and are perfect for many seasonal arrangements.

Growing Purchase roses from a catalog or your local nursery. Plant them in an area with full sun and plenty of air circulation. Amend the soil with peat moss or compost and a fertilizer formulated for roses. After planting, mulch your new rose bush and water it regularly.

Harvesting Harvest roses at any stage, from bud to full bloom, but they may shatter if picked too late.

Drying We dry roses and their foliage in silica gel because air-dried roses shrivel considerably. Cut the flower heads from their stems and place them upright in a container of silica gel. Lay the stems (with foliage attached) on their sides and cover with additional silica gel. Once dry, spray the blossoms and foliage with a sealer and colored floral sprays. Reattach the flower heads to their stems with hot glue. Dry small sprays of flowers and buds on their sides in a container of silica gel.

SALVIA HORMINUM
Clary Sage
Annual

>—•◇•—<

Color Pink, purple, white
Height 18 in. – 20 in.
Spacing 12 in.
Sowing Depth ⅛ in.
Germination Temp 70°F – 75°F
Germination Time 12 – 15 days

The brightly colored bracts of *Salvia horminum* air-dry easily and retain their vibrant hues. Use these colorful stems throughout your medium-size arrangements for small, vivid color spots. The multi-stemmed plants produce an abundance of arranging material while offering a beautiful garden display from midsummer on. In our garden (Zone 7), this easy-to-grow annual readily self-seeds if the pods are left to ripen.

Growing About 6 to 8 weeks before the last frost, sow the seeds in a soilless mix and lightly cover them with additional medium. Once they've germinated, transplant the seedlings to cell flats. After all danger of frost has passed, transplant them to a sunny location in the garden and keep the soil evenly moist.

Harvesting The stems are ready to harvest when the bracts have fully matured and feel firm to the touch. Cut the stems long; they can always be trimmed for a particular arrangement.

Drying Bundle several stems together with a rubber band and hang them upside down to dry.

SCABIOSA STELLATA
Starflower
Annual

>—•◇•—<

Color Seedpods: light brown
Height 24 in. – 36 in.
Spacing 12 in. – 16 in.
Sowing Depth ⅛ in.
Germination Temp 65°F – 70°F
Germination Time 7 – 12 days

Starflowers have white, pincushion flowers that turn into unique, light-brown seed heads. Their long stems give the plant a gangly appearance in the garden, but the spherical, papery seedpods add interesting texture to fall arrangements.

Growing About 2 to 3 weeks before the last frost, fill a cell flat with a soilless mix and place one seed in each cell. The seedlings will grow in the flat without further transplanting until it's time to plant them in the garden. After all danger of frost has passed, plant the seedlings in a sunny location.

Harvesting Once the flowers fade, watch the seed heads closely because they develop quickly. Harvest each seed head when it has fully developed into a sphere. They shatter if picked too late.

Drying Air-dried starflowers may shatter even if they were picked at the proper time, so it's best to preserve them with glycerin prior to air-drying. Once treated, bundle 5 or 6 stems together with a rubber band and hang them upside down to dry.

SENECIO CINERARIA
Dusty Miller
Annual

>─┼◆>─○─<◆┼─<

Color Silvery-gray
Height 6 in. – 12 in.
Spacing 8 in. – 10 in.
Sowing Depth Surface-sow
Germination Temp 65°F – 70°F
Germination Time 10 – 15 days

Dusty miller is typically grown as an annual, but in warm regions some species are perennial. Dusty miller's silvery foliage and compact form are perfectly suited for edging a path or defining a garden border. When used in winter arrangements, its fuzzy-textured foliage and light-gray color can evoke a frosty feeling.

Growing About 8 to 10 weeks before the last frost, fill a flat with soilless mix and sow the seeds on the surface. Once they've germinated and the seedlings are large enough to handle, transplant them to cell flats. After all danger of frost has passed, transplant them to a garden location with full sun and well-drained soil.

Harvesting Harvest the foliage in mid to late summer. Cut off the individual leaves, or harvest entire stems with the leaves attached.

Drying Place individual leaves on a drying rack (see pp. 39-40) and lightly press them beneath sections of newspaper. Once dry, attach clusters of the leaves to a wire or pick for use in arrangements. The leaves can also be used singly in wreaths and garlands. Dry entire stems (with leaves attached) in silica gel.

STACHYS BYZANTINA
(STACHYS LANATA)
Lamb's Ears
Perennial

>─┼◆>─○─<◆┼─<

Color Silvery-green
Height 12 in. – 18 in.
Spacing 9 in. – 12 in.
Sowing Depth Lightly cover
Germination Temp 65°F – 70°F
Germination Time 7 – 10 days

Lamb's ears is an appropriate name for a plant with soft and wooly leaves. Although lamb's ears produces lanky 12-in. to 18-in. flower spikes, it's the 4-in. leaves that we use in dried-flower arrangements. Whether used individually on wreaths or grouped in small clusters, lamb's ears soften the appearance of any seasonal arrangement.

Growing About 6 to 8 weeks before the last frost, sow the seeds in a soilless mix. Once the seeds germinate and the seedlings are large enough to handle, transplant them to cell flats. After all danger of frost has passed, transplant them to a garden location with full sun and average garden soil. Avoid overhead watering because it will mat the hairs on the leaves.

Harvesting Harvest the leaves when they are fully developed and in their prime. Old, damaged, or yellowing leaves are not appropriate for drying.

Drying Spread the individual leaves out on a drying rack (see pp. 39-40) in a warm, dark location.

SYRINGA
Lilac
Deciduous Shrub

>—+◆—○—◆+—<

Color Wine-red, lavender, purple, white
Height 6 ft. – 20 ft.
Spacing 10 ft. – 20 ft.
Planting Depth Same as container
Planting Time Spring
Harvest Time Spring

The delightfully heady fragrance from a lilac bush is a sure sign of spring. While you can't preserve the scent, the luxuriant blossoms can be dried in silica gel for enjoyment all year long. These large flowers are definitely focal-point material. The most common and readily available species is *Syringa vulgaris.*

Growing Purchase lilac plants from a catalog or your local nursery. Grow them in full sun or light shade in well-drained soil. Water regularly and fertilize in the spring.

Harvesting Harvest lilacs when they are in full bloom. Leave a short length of stem attached.

Drying Lay the blossoms on their sides and cover them with silica gel. Once dry, apply a surface sealer and colored floral sprays. Hot-glue the individual flowers onto wreaths or garlands. For use in arrangements, glue and tape wires to the stem ends (see p. 61).

TAGETES
Marigold
Annual

>—+◆—○—◆+—<

Color Maroon, orange, yellow
Height 8 in. – 36 in.
Spacing 10 in. – 12 in.
Sowing Depth ⅛ in.
Germination Temp 70°F – 75°F
Germination Time 5 – 14 days

Marigolds are extremely easy to grow, and their ruffled blooms add bright color spots to gardens as well as to arrangements. Varieties with large, fully double, carnation-like blooms, such as African marigolds *(Tagetes erecta)* or their hybrids, are best for drying. Marigolds air-dry easily and retain their bright colors. The ruffled petals help disguise the inevitable shriveling that occurs during the air-drying process.

Growing About 3 to 4 weeks before the last frost, sow the seeds in a soilless mix. Once germinated, transplant the seedlings to cell flats. After all danger of frost has passed, transplant them to a sunny location in the garden.

Harvesting Harvest the individual flower heads just as they reach full bloom. Mature flowers might look perfect, but they may shatter once harvested and dried.

Drying Air-dry marigold flower heads using the drying rack described on pp. 39-40. Alternately, dry them in silica gel for perfectly formed blooms. Once they are dry, glue the blossoms onto wires or dried surrogate stems (see pp. 61-63 for details).

TULIPA
Tulip
Bulb

⊱┈◈┈◦┈◈┈⊰

Color Pink, red, orange, yellow, purple, white
Height 12 in. – 30 in.
Spacing 4 in. – 6 in.
Planting Depth 4 in. – 8 in.
Planting Time Fall
Harvest Time Spring

Tulips give the spring landscape an elegant air, and they lend the same feeling to arrangements. It takes patience to dry and preserve their delicate petals, but the outcome is worth the effort.

Growing In the fall, purchase tulip bulbs from your local garden center or order them from a catalog during the summer. Choose an area of the garden with full sun and well-drained soil, then amend the soil with peat moss or compost, sand, and bone meal or bulb fertilizer. Plant the bulbs in late fall; they will bloom the following spring.

Harvesting Harvest the blooms before they fully open. Cut the stems 8 in. to 10 in. long and temporarily place them in a vase of water while you complete the following step.

Drying Once the flowers are cut, insert a wire into the stem and dry the blooms in silica gel (see p. 40-43 for details). When the flowers are dry, spray them with several light coats of a surface sealer. Because their delicate colors tend to fade, apply colored floral sprays.

ZINNIA ELEGANS
Zinnia
Annual

⊱┈◈┈◦┈◈┈⊰

Color Pink, rose, red, orange, yellow, purple, white
Height 10 in. – 36 in.
Spacing 10 in. – 20 in.
Sowing Depth ⅛ in.
Germination Temp 70°F – 75°F
Germination Time 5 – 7 days

Zinnias are available in a wide range of colors and sizes. With blooms up to 6 in. across, dahlia-flowered zinnias are striking focal points in large arrangements. The 2½-in. blooms of dwarf varieties are perfectly proportioned for smaller displays.

Growing About 2 to 3 weeks before the last frost, sow the seeds in a soilless mix. Once they've germinated, transplant the seedlings to cell flats. After all danger of frost has passed, transplant them to a garden location with full sun and well-drained soil.

Harvesting Harvest zinnias in full bloom. Cut the flowers from their stems, leaving about 1 in. of stem attached to each flower head.

Drying Place the flower heads face up in a container of silica gel, then cover the blooms with additional silica gel. When dry, glue the flowers either onto wires, surrogate stems, or directly onto wreaths and garlands. Zinnias retain their natural colors fairly well, but we suggest applying several light coats of a surface sealer and colored floral sprays.

RED (MAROON)

Amaranth
(Amaranthus)

Anemone
(Anemone coronaria)

Aster
(Callistephus chinensis)

Celosia
(Celosia argentea)

Dahlia *(Dahlia)*

Flossflower
(Ageratum houstonianum)

Globe amaranth
(Gomphrena)

Hellebore
(Helleborus)

Hollyhock
(Alcea rosea)

Lilac *(Syringa)*

Lily *(Lilium)*

Marigold *(Tagetes)*

Orach
(Atriplex hortensis)

Ornamental grasses

Peony *(Paeonia)*

Rose *(Rosa)*

Snapdragon
(Anthirrhinum majus)

Strawflower
(Helichrysum bracteatum)

Tulip *(Tulipa)*

Yarrow *(Achillea)*

Zinnia
(Zinnia elegans)

PINK (ROSE)

Aster
(Callistephus chinensis)

Celosia
(Celosia argentea)

Clary
(Salvia horminum)

Dahlia *(Dahlia)*

Dogwood *(Cornus)*

Globe amaranth
(Gomphrena)

Hollyhock
(Alcea rosea)

Hyacinth
(Hyacinthus)

Larkspur
(Consolida)

Lily *(Lilium)*

Peony *(Paeonia)*

Rose *(Rosa)*

Rose beauty
(Helichrysum cassianum)

Russian statice
(Limonium suworowii)

Snapdragon
(Anthirrhinum majus)

Statice
(Limonium sinuatum)

Strawflower
(Helichrysum bracteatum)

Wheat celosia
(Celosia argentea var. spicata)

Yarrow *(Achillea)*

Zinnia
(Zinnia elegans)

PEACH (APRICOT)

Hollyhock
(Alcea rosea)

Hyacinth
(Hyacinthus)

Lily *(Lilium)*

Rose *(Rosa)*

Statice
(Limonium sinuatum)

Strawflower
(Helichrysum bracteatum)

Yarrow *(Achillea)*

ORANGE

Celosia
(Celosia argentea)

Chinese lantern
(Physalis alkekengi)

Dahlia
(Dahlia)

Gladwin iris
(Iris foetidissima)

Globe amaranth
(Gomphrena)

Lily *(Lilium)*

Marigold *(Tagetes)*

Rose *(Rosa)*

Safflower
(Carthamus tinctorius)

Snapdragon
(Anthirrhinum majus)

Strawflower
(Helichrysum bracteatum)

Sunflowers
(Helianthus annuus)

Tulip *(Tulipa)*

Yarrow *(Achillea)*

Zinnia *(Zinnia elegans)*

YELLOW (YELLOW-GREEN)

Aster
(Callistephus chinensis)

Celosia
(Celosia argentea)

Daffodil
(Narcissus)

Dahlia *(Dahlia)*

Drumstick
(Craspedia globosa)

Hellebore
(Helleborus)

Hollyhock
(Alcea rosea)

Hyacinth
(Hyacinthus)

Knapweed
(Centaurea macrocephala)

Lady's mantle
(Alchemilla mollis)

Lily *(Lilium)*

Marigold *(Tagetes)*

Rose *(Rosa)*

Snapdragon
(Anthirrhinum majus)

Statice
(Limonium sinuatum)

Strawflower
(Helichrysum bracteatum)

Sunflowers
(Helianthus annuus)

Tulip *(Tulipa)*

Yarrow *(Achillea)*

Zinnia
(Zinnia elegans)

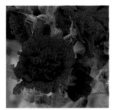
Hollyhock

Wheat celosia

Hyacinth

Chinese lantern

Lady's mantle

GREEN (GRAY-GREEN)

Amaranth
(Amaranthus)

Bells of Ireland
(Moluccella laevis)

Dusty miller
(Senecio cineraria)

Gum tree
(Eucalyptus)

Hellebore
(Helleborus)

Hop
(Humulus Lupulus)

Lamb's Ears
(Stachys byzantina)

Love-in-a-mist
(Nigella)

Money plant
(Lunaria annua)

Orach
(Atriplex hortensis)

Oregano
(Origanum vulgare)

Ornamental grasses

Sea holly *(Eryngium)*

BLUE

Aster
(Callistephus chinensis)

Delphinium
(Delphinium)

Globe thistle
(Echinops)

Hyacinth
(Hyacinthus)

Hydrangea
(Hydrangea)

Larkspur *(Consolida)*

Love-in-a-mist
(Nigella)

Sea holly *(Eryngium)*

Statice
(Limonium sinuatum)

PURPLE (VIOLET)

Anemone
(Anemone coronaria)

Aster
(Callistephus chinensis)

Cardoon
(Cynara cardunculus)

Clary
(Salvia horminum)

Dahlia *(Dahlia)*

Delphinium
(Delphinium)

Flossflower
(Ageratum houstonianum)

Gayfeather
(Liatris spicata)

Globe amaranth
(Gomphrena)

Hyacinth
(Hyacinthus)

Hydrangea
(Hydrangea)

Larkspur *(Consolida)*

Lilac *(Syringa)*

Oregano
(Origanum vulgare)

Rose *(Rosa)*

Sea lavender
(Limonium latifolium)

Statice
(Limonium sinuatum)

Yarrow *(Achillea)*

Zinnia
(Zinnia elegans)

BEIGE (BROWN)

Coneflower
(Echinacea purpurea)

Orach
(Atriplex hortensis)

Ornamental grasses

Poppy
(Papaver somniferum)

Starflower
(Scabiosa stellata)

WHITE (CREAM)

Aster
(Callistephus chinensis)

Baby's breath
(Gypsophila paniculata)

Bishop's weed
(Ammi)

Clary
(Salvia horminum)

Dahlia *(Dahlia)*

Dogwood *(Cornus)*

Globe amaranth
(Gomphrena)

Hyacinth
(Hyacinthus)

Larkspur
(Consolida)

Lilac *(Syringa)*

Lily *(Lilium)*

Rose *(Rosa)*

Safflower
(Carthamus tinctorius)

Snapdragon
(Anthirrhinum majus)

Statice
(Limonium sinuatum)

Strawflower
(Helichrysum bracteatum)

Tulip *(Tulipa)*

Wax-leaf privet
(Ligustrum japonicum)

Winged everlasting
(Ammobium alatum)

Zinnia
(Zinnia elegans)

Sea holly

Love-in-a-mist

Gayfeather

Starflower

German statice

APPENDIX TWO other plants for drying

PARTS OF THE PLANT TO DRY	BEST DRYING METHOD
= Flower	= Silica gel
= Foliage	= Hang-dry
= Seed heads	= Flat-dry
	= Glycerin

🍃⌒	Angle's-Fishing-Rods	*Dierama pendulum*
✾🍃⌒	Artemesia	*Artemesia ludoviciana*
✾✳	Astilbe	*Astilbe* (various species)
🍃◊	Beech	*Fagus sylvatica*
🍃⌒◊	Boxwood	*Buxus* (various species)
✾✳	Calendula, Pot Marigold	*Calendula officinalis*
✾✳	Carnations, Pinks, Sweet William	*Dianthus* (various species)
⋎⌒	Corn, Ornamental	*Zea mays*
✾✳⌒	Feverfew	*Chrysanthemum parthenium*
⋎⌒	Fibigia, Roman Shields	*Fibigia clypeata*
✾⋎⌒	Globe Artichoke	*Cynara scolymus*
✾⌒	Helipterum	*Helipterum roseum*
🍃⌒◊	Holly	*Ilex aquifolium*
✾⌒	Immortelle	*Xeranthemum annuum*
🍃✳◊	Ivy	*Hedera helix*
🍃▤	Japanese Iris	*Iris kaempferi*
✾⌒	Lavender	*Lavandula* (various species)
✾✳	Lily-of-the-Valley	*Convallaria majalis*

			Magnolia, Southern	*Magnolia grandiflora*
Monkshood	*Aconitum* (various species)
Montebretia	*Crocosmia* (various species)
Noble Fir	*Abies procera*
Oregon Grape	*Mahonia aquifolium*
Pansy	*Viola x wittrockiana*
Pepper, Ornamental	*Capsicum annuum*
Peppergrass	*Lepidium parthenium*
Salal	*Gaultheria shallon*
Salvia	*Salvia farinacea*
Scotch Broom	*Cytisus scoparius*
Shoo-Fly Plant	*Nicandra physalodes*
Silver Thistle	*Carlina acaulis*
Veronica	*Veronica spicata*
Willow, Curly or Dragon Claw	*Salix matsudana* 'Tortusa'

A

Amaranth (*Amaranthus*)
Anemone, poppy-flowered (*Anemone coronaria*)
Aster (*Callistephus chinensis*)

B

Baby's breath (*Gypsophila paniculata*)
Bells of Ireland (*Moluccella laevis*)
Bishop's weed (*Ammi*)
Blazing star (*Liatris spicata*)

C

Cardoon (*Cynara cardunculus*)
Celosia, plumed (*Celosia argentea*)
Celosia, wheat (*Celosia argentea var. spicata*)
Chinese lantern (*Physalis alkekengi*)
Clary (*Salvia horminum*)
Cockscomb (*Celosia argentea*)
Coneflower, purple (*Echinacea purpurea*)

D

Daffodil (*Narcissus*)
Dahlia (*Dahlia*)
Delphinium (*Delphinium*)
Dogwood (*Cornus*)
Drumstick (*Craspedia globosa*)
Dusty miller (*Senecio cineraria*)

F

Flossflower (*Ageratum houstonianum*)

G

Gayfeather (*Liatris spicata*)
German statice (*Limonium [Goniolimon] tataricum*)
Globe amaranth (*Gomphrena*)
Globe thistle (*Echinops*)
Gum tree (*Eucalyptus*)

H

Hellebore (*Helleborus*)
Hollyhock (*Alcea rosea*)
Honesty (*Lunaria annua*)
Hop (*Humulus lupulus*)
Hyacinth (*Hyacinthus*)
Hydrangea (*Hydrangea*)

I

Iris, gladwin (*Iris foetidissima*)
Iris, scarlet-seeded (*Iris foetidissima*)

K

Knapweed (*Centaurea macrocephala*)

L

Lady's mantle (*Alchemilla mollis*)
Lamb's ears (*Stachys byzantina [S. lanata]*)
Larkspur (*Consolida*)
Lilac (*Syringa*)
Lily (*Lilium*)
Love-in-a-mist (*Nigella*)

M

Marigold (*Tagetes*)
Money plant (*Lunaria annua*)

O

Orach (*Atriplex hortensis*)
Oregano (*Origanum vulgare*)
Ornamental grasses

P

Peony (*Paeonia*)
Poppy (*Papaver somniferum*)
Privet, wax-leaf (*Ligustrum japonicum*)

R

Rose (*Rosa*)
Rose beauty (*Helichrysum cassianum*)

S

Safflower (*Carthamus tinctorius*)
Sea holly (*Eryngium*)
Sea lavender (*Limonium latifolium*)
Silver dollar (*Lunaria annua*)
Snapdragon (*Anthirrhinum majus*)
Starflower (*Scabiosa stellata*)
Statice (*Limonium sinuatum*)
Statice, Russian (*Limonium* or *Psyilliostachys suworowii*)
Strawflower (*Helichrysum bracteatum*)
Sunflowers (*Helianthus annuus*)

T

Tulip (*Tulipa*)

W

Winged everlasting (*Ammobium alatum*)

Y

Yarrow (*Achillea*)

Z

Zinnia (*Zinnia elegans*)

SEEDS

Chiltern Seeds
Bortree Stile, Ulverston
Cumbria LA12 7PB
England
Phone: Ulverston (01229) 581137
Fax: (01229) 584549
www.edirectory.co.uk/chilternseeds

Comstock, Ferre & Co.
263 Main St.
Wethersfield, CT 06109
Phone: (860) 571-6590
Fax: (860) 571-6595
www.tiac.net/users/comstock

Ferry-Morse Seeds
P. O. Box 488
Fulton, KY 42041-0488
Phone: (800) 283-6400
Fax: (800) 283-2700
www.ferry-morse.com

Gurney's
110 Capital St.
Yankton, SD 57079
Phone: (605) 665-1671
Fax: (605) 665-9718

J. W. Seed Co.
335 S. High St.
Randolph, WI 53957-0001
Phone: (800) 247-5864
Fax: (800) 692-5864

Johnny's Selected Seeds
Foss Hill Rd.
Albion, ME 04910-9731
Phone: (207) 437-4301
Fax: (800) 437-4290
www.johnnysselectedseeds.com

Nichols Garden Nursery
1190 N. Pacific Highway N.E.
Albany, OR 97321-4580
Phone: (541) 928-9280
Fax: (541) 967-8406
www.gardennursery.com

Otis S. Twilley Seed Co.
121 Gary Rd.
Hodges, SC 29653
Phone: (800) 622-7333
Fax: (215) 245-1949

Park Seed Co., Inc.
1 Parkton Ave.
Greenwood, SC 29647-0001
Phone: (800) 845-3369
Fax: (800) 275-9941
www.parkseed.com

R. H. Shumway's
P. O. Box 1
Graniteville, SC 29829-0001
Phone: (803) 663-9771
Fax: (888) 437-2733

Seymour's Select Seeds
P. O. Box 1346
Sussex, VA 23884-0346
Phone: (803) 663-3084
Fax: (888) 739-6687

Shepherd's Garden Seeds
30 Irene St.
Torrington, CT 06790-6658
Phone: (860) 482-3638
Fax: (860) 482-0532
www.shepherdseeds.com

Stokes
P. O. Box 548
Buffalo, NY 14240-0548
Phone: (716) 695-6980
Fax: (888) 834-3334
www.stokeseeds.com

Thompson & Morgan Inc.
P. O. Box 1308
Jackson, NJ 08527-0308
Phone: (800) 274-7333
Fax: (888) 466-4769
www.thompson-morgan.com

W. Atlee Burpee & Co.
300 Park Ave.
Warminster, PA 18991-0001
Phone: (800) 888-1447
Fax: (800) 487-5530
www.burpee.com

BULBS

Breck's
6523 N. Galena Rd.
Peoria, IL 61632
Phone: (800) 722-9069
Fax: (800) 996-2852
www.brecks.com

Dutch Gardens
P. O. Box 200
Adelphia, NJ 07710-0200
Phone: (800) 818-3861
Fax: (732) 780-7720
www.dutchgardens.nl/home.htm

Holland Bulb Farms
423 Broad St.
P. O. Box 220
Tatamy, PA 18085-0220
Phone: (800) 283-5082
Fax: (610) 253-9012

John Scheepers, Inc.
23 Tulip Dr.
Bantam, CT 06750
Phone: (860) 567-0838
Fax: (860) 567-5323

The Lily Garden
P. O. Box 407
La Center, WA 98629
Phone/Fax: (360) 263-5588

Van Dyck's Flower Farms, Inc.
P. O. Box 430
Brightwaters, NY 11718-0430
Phone: (800) 248-2852
Fax: (516) 669-3518
www.vandycks.com

Van Lierop Bulb Farm, Inc.
13407 80th St. E.
Puyallup, WA 98372-3608
Phone: (253) 848-7272
Fax: (253) 848-9142

PLANTS

Inter-State Nurseries
1800 Hamilton Rd.
Bloomington, IL 61704-9609
Phone: (309) 663-9551

Jackson & Perkins
1 Rose Ln.
Medford, OR 97501-0702
Phone: (800) 292-4769
Fax: (800) 242-0329
www.jacksonandperkins.com

Spring Hill
6523 N. Galena Rd.
Peoria, IL 61632
Phone: (800) 582-8527
Fax: (800) 991-2852
www.springhillnursery.com

GARDEN SUPPLIES

A. M. Leonard, Inc.
P. O. Box 816
241 Fox Dr.
Piqua, OH 45356
Phone: (800) 543-8955
Fax: (800) 433-0633
www.amleo.com

Charley's Greenhouse Supply
17979 State Route 536
Mount Vernon, WA 98273
Phone: (800) 322-4707
Fax: (800) 233-3078
www.charleysgreenhouse.com

Gardener's Supply Company
128 Intervale Rd.
Burlington, VT 05401-2850
Phone: (800) 863-1700
Fax: (800) 551-6712
www.gardeners.com

Gardens Alive!
5100 Schenley Pl.
Lawrenceburg, IN 47025
Phone: (812) 537-8651
Fax: (812) 537-5108
www.gardens-alive.com

Mellinger's, Inc.
2310 W. South Range Rd.
North Lima, OH 44452-9731
Phone: (800) 321-7444
Fax: (330) 549-3716
www.mellingers.com

Stillbrook Horticultural Supplies
P. O. Box 600
Bantam, CT 06750
Phone: (800) 414-4468
Fax: (860) 567-5323

GREENHOUSE KITS

Stokes
address/phone number on p. 207

Charley's Greenhouse Supply
address/phone number at left